TWO SNOWDONIA RIVERS

Glaslyn & Dwyryd

PHOTOGRAPHY
JEAN NAPIER

TEXT
ALUN JOHN RICHARDS

First published: 2008

© Photography: Jean Napier   Text: Alun John Richards

ISBN: 978-1-84527-206-7

Published by
Gwasg Carreg Gwalch,
12 Iard yr Orsaf, Llanrwst, Wales, LL26 0EH.
Tel: 01492 642031 Fax: 01492 641502
e-mail: llyfrau@carreg-gwalch.co.uk
www.carreg-gwalch.co.uk

Printed in Malta by Progress Press Co. Ltd

Jean Napier ARPS

Born in East London, Jean Napier has lived in the Snowdonia National Park since 1991 and the magnificent scenery is the main inspiration for her photography. Man's influences on the landscape of Wales are a recurring theme in her exhibitions and photography books and her first book *Rhosydd A Personal View – Golwg Bersonol* (bilingual Welsh/English) depicts the remains of an old slate quarry in northern Wales with historical text.

Her primary motivation is to promote photography as an art form, to show the versatility and creativity of the photographic image; that it is not just a method of 'recording' moments. Her work has been exhibited throughout the UK, in the USA and Australia.

She runs photographic workshops with students of all ages and abilities throughout the UK and is a tutor for the Open College of Art. She holds a BA Honours Degree in Photographic Studies and is an Associate of the Royal Photographic Society.

More information and a gallery available on: www.jean-napier.com

Alun John Richards

A retired engineer who for many years was a guest tutor at the Snowdonia National Park Environmental Studies Centre, Plas Tan y Bwlch and sometime lecturer at Coleg Harlech Summer Schools.

A native of Swansea he is a past Chairman of the South West Wales Industrial Archaeology Society and of the Swansea Art Society

Although his speciality is the Welsh slate industry on which he is an acknowledged expert, he also writes and lectures on a variety of aspects of industrial history.

He is also a vigorous defender of the landscape and environment of Wales.

More information and book list on: www.richards-slate.co.uk

Foreword

Yng nghesail Eryri in *Cymraeg* – the middle element of which conveys: 'snuggling under the arm of a loved one' – is a neater description, free from the connotations of its English equivalent which locates, mapwise, the Glaslyn and Dwyryd rivers 'in the armpit of Snowdonia'! Such an analogy, nevertheless, evokes the pivotal geographical and strategic position commanded by these two rivers which become conjoined in the magnificent sands separating Harlech from Morfa Bychan. What a truly dramatic sight it must have been before the Glaslyn's incarceration by Madocks' Cob in 1812.

Like the lives of ancient heroes no other Welsh rivers make more dramatic, if short, journeys than these two. The Glaslyn's narrow and gloriously rugged, lake-strung upper catchment includes the eastern summit slope of Yr Wyddfa (Snowdon), only 12 miles upstream, while the broad sweep of the Dwyryd's numerous tributaries are noted for squeezing through some ridiculously narrow gorges and over some truly imposing cataracts.

However, there's far more behind the awesome scenic context of these watery peregrinations, so evocatively captured by Jean's lens, than meets the eye. Are there not voices emanating from the gushing waters? And can we not tune in to what they tell of the legends, tales and experiences of those who came before us – monks, miners, saints, shepherds, quarrymen, heroes, sinners, smugglers and many more? It is their stories that Alun's bubbling prose presents to us, as a cornucopia of cultural heritage to colour, enrich and enliven our river journeys from source to sea.

Twm Elias
Ionawr 23ain, 2008

Introduction

The waters of the two rivers, the Glaslyn and the Dwyryd, rise and flow through land where mankind has lived, hunted and cultivated for a thousand generations. A land permeated by fable and folk tale that has seen invaders and incursors come and go; a land that has been bent and moulded but not broken by adversity.

A land of churches and saints that almost predate popes and prelates, where Christian beliefs become compounded with heathen custom and legend. A land of patriots and poets where a verse is more valued than a jewel, and a song is an accompaniment to every happening.

Neither river is as wide as the Amazon nor as long as the Nile but each offers a charm, a beauty and an ambience in the very heartland of Wales.

Both rivers originate in mountain lakes high above their ultimate valleys, the Glaslyn publicly and spectacularly, the Dwyryd a little more discreetly. The Glaslyn does work for its living but in one spectacular 'job and finish' endeavour that then leaves it free to pursue the rest of its journey at leisure. The Dwyryd leaves all toil to its leated and laundered tributaries but also provides their waters with eventual tranquillity.

To compare the two rivers takes one into 'Apples versus Oranges' territory. The Glaslyn might claim that Nantgwynant, Cwm Hafod y Llan, Aberglaslyn Gorge and the lakes, entitle it to precedence. Against this the Dwyryd can claim more waterfalls, the glowering Migneint, the Vale of Maentwrog and Llandecwyn churchyard.

In truth these rivers are incomparable.

Dedicated to all who helped to make this book possible and particularly to the late Merfyn Williams whose devotion to his country and its countryside was matched only by his ability to inspire equal devotion to them in others

Previous Books

JEAN NAPIER

Rhosydd A Personal View – Golwg Bersonol   IBSN 978-0-86381-470-0
A Tale of Two Rivers (with Alun John Richards)   IBSN 978-0-86381-989-3

ALUN JOHN RICHARDS

A Gazeteer of the Welsh Slate Industry   IBSN 978-0-86381-196-5
Slate Quarrying at Corris   IBSN 978-0-86381-279-1
Slate Quarrying in Wales   IBSN 978-0-86381-319-4
Slate Quarrying in Pembrokeshire   IBSN 978-0-86381-484-0
The Slate Regions of North& Mid Wales   IBSN 978-0-86381-552-9
The Slate Railways of Wales   IBSN 978-0-86381-689-4
Fragments of Mine and Mill   IBSN 978-0-86381-812-9
Cwm Gwyrfai (with Gwynfor Pierce Jones)   IBSN 978-0-86381-987-8
Welsh Slate Craft   IBSN 978-1-84527-029-9
Crefftwyr Llechi   IBSN 978-1-84527-034-7
Slate Quarrying in Wales (Revised)   IBSN 978-1-84527-026-6
Published by Gwasg Carreg Gwalch, Llanrwst, Wales

Gazeteer of Slate Quarrying in Wales   IBSN 978-1-84524-074-X
Slate Quarrying in Corris   IBSN 978-1-84524-068-5
Published by Llygad Gwalch, Llwyndyrys, Wales

Contents

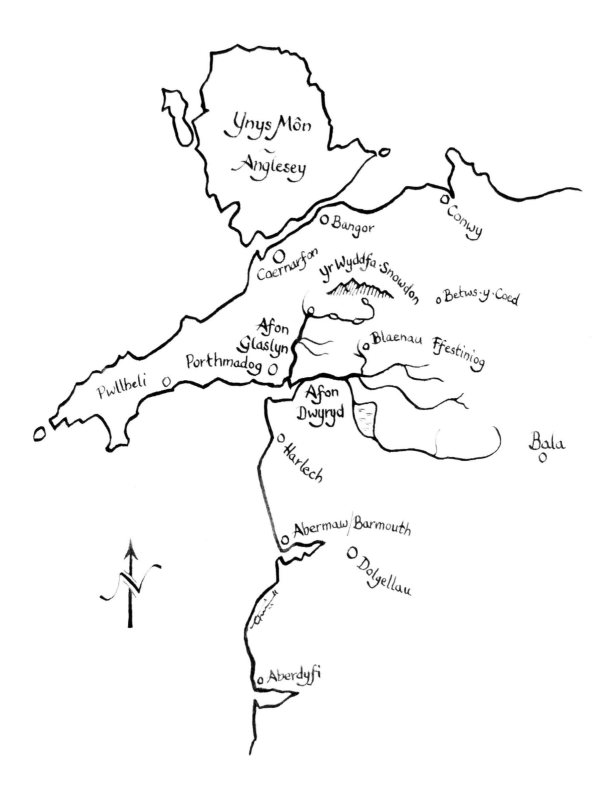

GLASLYN

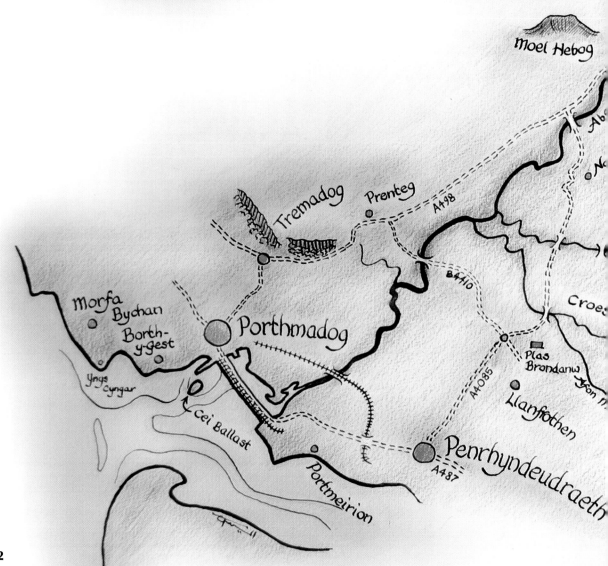

Llyn·y·Gader

ge

Colwyn

Yr Wyddfa / Snowdon

Beddgelert

Glaslyn

Dinas Emrys

Llyn
Llydaw

Pen·y·Pass

Gelert's
grave

Gladstone
Rock

Pen·y·
Gwryd

Sygun
Copper mine

Llyn Dinas

Afon Glaslyn

Moel y Dyniewyd

Llyn Gwynant

A498

Nanmor

yr Arddu

Llyn Llagi

Cnicht

Llyn yr Adar

Afon Croesor

Llyn Croesor

Moelwyn

GLASLYN
1
THE SOURCE

Almost at the very apogee of Snowdon the emotional epicentre of all Welsh people under the glowering crag of Garnedd Ugain a thousand spermatazodic oozings form the eponymous lake that is the womb of the Glaslyn river. Of the 25 lakes said to be visible from the top of Snowdon, Llyn Glaslyn is one of the largest but not the highest, this is Ffynnon Llyffant in the Carneddau that tops Glaslyn by almost 1000 feet, although purists might claim that being well under the geographer's two hectare minimum for lake status, it should be classed as a mere pond, but to demean any of Snowdon's lakes with the appellation of a village duckery is a travesty that should be shunned.

Originally called Llyn Ffynnon Glas, it was probably contracted to its present form *'green lake'* in the early 19th century by the Britannia miners, its colour deriving from the ore that provided the copper for the bronze of Nelsonian cannon. Around and above the lake the hillside is so comprehensively tunnelled that it would seem to be in imminent danger of collapsing like a termited chair-leg.

Cuprous pollution effectively sterilises the lake's dark waters, but in pre-industrial times there were tales of strange fish being lured from unfathomable profundities. Like every lake in Wales of more than wadeable depth it was described as 'bottomless' and having its resident Afanc, a fearsome creature that snatched sheep, goats and any humans foolish enough to approach the water's edge. Having avoided the dreaded Afanc and escaped the capricious Tylwyth Teg, one might find oneself enriched with silver coin by mysterious lake-dwelling maidens. Such bounty could prove ephemeral, since if one made any virtue-threatening overtures, boasted of one's fiscal fortune or did anything else that offended the maidens, all goods bought with it and any coin unspent immediately turned to worthless dross.

Although ornithologists say that no eagles have been sighted since the 17th century, few doubt that the White Eagle of Snowdonia maintains its unseen guardianship of this inner donjon of Eryri.

Today the lakeside once skirted by the ore trucks' rails, provides a flask and sandwich break for Gortexed walkers striving for a digitally-captured summit snap or booted botanists seeking the now vanishing *Lloydia Serotina*, the Snowdon Lily, the Edelweiss of Wales whose naming honoured the great 17th century naturalist, Edward Lhuyd.

However, this was once where the ore-carriers paused for a hand-scooped drink of its waters before hefting their weighty sacks and zigzagging their way up to the summit's shoulder, from where their product could be sledged down to the Llyn Peris barges. This onerous task was obviated in the mid-19th century by the building of the aptly named 'Miners Track' up from Pen y Pass.

From here, the river plunges with a childish eagerness to blend into Llyn Llydaw one of the largest and deepest corrie lakes of Snowdonia. The discovery of oak dugout canoes confirmed ancient navigation; in fact, until a causeway was built across the lake, ore was rafted across it. All year round the causeway carries an endless ant-like crocodile of Snowdon-bound ramblers rejoicing in the thousand-foot advantage that the Pen y Pass route has over the Watkin Path. Like its elder sister Llyn Glaslyn, the Llydaw bears no fish, polluted by the detritus of the late 19th century river-driven crusher-rollers, stamps and sieves that processed ore brought by ropeway from the mines above. Part of a stamp box whose robustness defied the scrappies' hammers is still to be seen. Bizarrely, it was

planned to smelt copper on this bleak site using peat as fuel.

Below, close alongside Llyn Teyrn that provided its 'En-suite' facilities are the remnants of the barracks, the weeklong home for the miners from Beddgelert and beyond. Lying in their dank, flea-pit beds, the chill winds knifing through the walls, they could listen for the nocturnal 'knockers', the mythical beings who by means of séance-like tappings would guide them to the richest veins.

The outfall of this small lake joins the Glaslyn river for its thousand-foot career into the valley below in spectacular cascades unfortunately attenuated by much of the water being enslaved into the feed pipe of the Cwm Dyli power station. Deplored by many, this pioneering installation nevertheless has for a century made its contribution to the lives and livelihoods of north-western Wales. Though its output is relatively trifling, it matches at a fraction of the cost that of dozens of the windmills that desecrate our mountains.

United with waters escaping from the power station's evil clutches and making common cause with Afon Trawsnant, the Glaslyn encounters its first bridge whose creation is attributed to the Romans as are seemingly most structures more than a few centuries old. The river rushes on to Llyn Gwynant to savour the tranquilly of the Nantgwynant valley, whose *Green pastures and quiet waters* could well have been the inspiration for the twenty-third psalm.

An ancient thoroughfare, Nantgwynant slices boldly through the Snowdon Massif and ever since the retreat of the glaciers that moulded it, its sheltered fields have yielded crops and its slopes provided rich grazing. Little wonder that it has been eagerly seized upon and settled by successive invaders. Fortunately a more recent invader was repulsed – the Electricity Board. Intent in 1950 on drowning this and five other Welsh valleys for hydro schemes, its minions were routed by a display of people power unseen since the storming of the Bastille.

Hafoding, the summer bag and baggage transhumanance to the higher pastures, has long ceased, nowadays just the stock is moved, but this old custom probably persisted in this valley longer than anywhere else. The traditional autumn pooling of labour to bring the sheep off the mountain still continues but it is not such a social occasion; for one thing less cider is quaffed since while a horse could be depended upon to carry its rider home in safety, similar reliance cannot be vested in a quad bike.

Although many old customs are no longer observed a few, such as the Mari Llwyd where the decorated horse's head is paraded from door to door is being revived. One ancient custom unlikely to be revived is bundling or courting in bed. The motorcar having enabled such matters to be conducted out of hearing of a stoat-eared mother, one presumes that this 18th century comment may no longer apply. – *Should the lover offer any indecency, then his mistress would fly from him with the velocity of light, his company would be shunned and should any lass be prevailed upon to accept his visits, her continentcy would be considered in doubt.*

In one way Nantgwynant is world-famous even before it is actually reached for just beyond the extremities of its cwm is the Pen y Gwyryd Hotel. Awash with mountaineering memorabilia, it has played host to Hilary and Tensing and innumerable distinguished climbers and is so entwined with Everest exploration as to be almost Nepalese territory.

However in the 19th century Nantgwynant was definitely the territory of the Vawdreys, a dynasty of divines who, besides building Plas Gwynant, also re-built the reputedly Roman Bryn Gwynant as a sort of grand holiday chalet, and devoted themselves to quarrelling with each other over the rights to the mineral riches that they fervently believed to lie beneath their land. Despite its owners' clerical credentials, the Plas was troubled by a destructive ghost that even a professional exorcist was unable to lay. It eventually vanished; reputedly to lurk at the bottom of Llyn Gwynant, ready to resume its hauntings at some unspecified later date.

This lake, unlike Glaslyn and Llydaw, does support fish but its trout are allegedly disappointingly adept at distinguishing a wisp of feather from more nourishing and less perilous fare.

GLASLYN
2
HAFOD Y LLAN

The Glaslyn is bridged at Pont Bethania, where the torrents of Afon Cwmllan merge. The nearby chapel that gives it its name served miners and quarrymen, since here the bucolic tranquillity of Nantgwynant's meadows was overtaken by industry.

High in the near-vertical Cwmllan valley, is Hafod y Llan slate quarry that in the 1860s caught the eye of a curiously christened wine and spirits merchant Lemon Hart. Mr. Hart like many before him and even more after him imagined that owning a slate quarry would bring riches that would make Croesus seem like a benefit claimant.

Mr. H might have been foolish but he was not stupid and realised that this treasure could not be unlocked while product had to be carried to Porthmadog by clanking, traction engine-drawn carts. However this would not be a problem since the latest of many schemes to run a railway along the valley from the new railway station at Porthmadog was clearly about to come to fruition.

How to efficiently carry the slates down the precipitous track to the valley floor railway without half of them being reduced to fragments remained a poser. With a boldness that had made his rum the market leader and the main brace of Her Majesty's fleet Mr. Hart planned, built and financed a tramway incline layout of unprecedentedly epic proportions. This would enable slate wagons to be lowered to the valley floor where they could be attached to the trains that would imminently be busily puffing up and down Nantgwynant with the regularity of a long-case clock. Thus product

would be unloaded on Porthmadog docks unsullied and unbroken a mere hour or so since being stowed on the heights of Snowdon.

Only of course it did not happen like that, the inclines were built but not the railway and Mr. Hart waited in vain for the engine's whistle to echo through the valley. The quarry's inaccessibility, combined with a reluctance of men to live and work where rainfall is measured not in inches but in yards and winter

wind speeds are quoted in miles per minute, have left the tramway as a magnificent industrial monument.

Slate quarrying was not the only nor even the first industry in Cwm Llan; copper mining is much older, although not necessarily more successful. One mine, Braich yr Onnen is high above the western side of the Llan valley with Hafod y Llan mine equally high to the east. Both sent material via ore slides to a shared mill, the ruins of which still remain close by their millpond where one of the very few runs of stone-block tramway sleepers is to be found in northwest Wales. Puzzlingly, part of the run appears so steep as to require rope working which the curvature would seem to preclude.

To the east eerily isolated at the head of Cwm Erch is the Llywydd mine, ruins of whose Afon Erch-powered mill contain machinery whose remoteness has enabled it to defy even the most assiduous scrap merchant. Like other copper mines on the Glaslyn, it sought to fill the void left by the decline of the great Anglesey mines, although more successful than most, its small scale and near Mediaeval methods could not compete with the Chilean and Cuban producers that by the later 19th century overwhelmed British output.

The end of slate and of copper did not allow the Afon Cwm Llan to resume its unhindered tumble; its power now drives a tiny electricity station.

Bethania chapel, houses a café so that the sustenance it now dispenses to those embarking on the assault of the Snowdon summit via the Watkin path, is of a corporal rather than a spiritual nature. Nearby is Hafod y Llan farmhouse more than 3000 feet below the farm's highest point whose steepness gives it a surface acreage notably larger than its cartographic extent.

The Watkin path was built by Sir Edward Watkin M.P., railway builder and philanthropist, and inaugurated by Sir William Gladstone in the presence of 2000 persons in 1892. The ceremony took place at Gladstone Rock, close to the slate workings and to the war-torn Plas Cwm Llan, the bleak barn of a house where quarry managers' wives understandably refused to live. The Rock bears a plaque that condescendingly refers to the singing of *Cymric Hymns and The Land of My Fathers*. (Hen Wlad Fy Nhadau having been accoladed a National Anthem seven years previously).

Gladstone, no doubt anxious to demonstrate a willingness to face hardship and peril, made part of his journey to Nantgwynant via the North Wales Narrow Gauge Railway. The special coach he used is now at Porthmadog Welsh Highland Station, in 2005 its first post-restoration passenger being his namesake great-grandson, Sir William Gladstone.

An early 19th century description of Nantgwynant refers to its – *Thriving plantations and elegant villas.* Undoubtedly accurate, but a miner's home was contemporaneously spoken of as having - *Filth and dirtiness that can better be imagined than described; a worm eaten bed, two small stools, and a table fixed to the wall, comprised the whole of his furniture' the smoke of the fire ascended through a small hole in the roof. The door did not appear proof against the 'churlish chiding of the winter blast'.*

This indicates how wretched were the lives of even comparatively high earners, as miners certainly were compared with farm workers. The imputation of slovenliness is unfair, since it makes no allowance for the problems of cleaning an earth-floored, chimneyless shack. We can be sure that the housewife would care for her few pathetic sticks of furniture as assiduously as any great lady in the grandest of mansions would cherish a Louis XIV cabinet. In any case, with an ill-fitting door inviting their nocturnal visits, the Tylwyth Teg would be quick to punish any housekeeping shortcomings.

Like most of the remoter parts of Wales Cwm Llan has its legends. It is said that a shepherd heard the plaintive cries of a creature trapped in a crevice. He succeeded in rescuing what he found to be a fairy or Tylwyth Teg child. Later he was approached by two men who announced that they were the guardians of the child and having thanked the shepherd for his kindness took the child and gave him an ornate shepherd's crook. Thereafter every year, every ewe bore twin ewe lambs making him very wealthy.

One night trying to cross the flooded river Cwm Llan, at the very place where there is now a nice slate-slab bridge, he missed his footing and in saving himself from the rushing torrent lost the crook. In the morning every one of his sheep had vanished, apparently for his having been so careless with the costly gift. Presumably the crook was partly of metal since metal generally figures in these legends that are thought to be allegories for the dramatic impact of metalworking invaders on stone-based communities. Right up to the 18th century and even later, the blacksmith was the most respected and best rewarded of tradesmen, practising as he did, a mysterious and arcane profession, his ability to dominate such a recalcitrant material and his fearless use of fire imputing some kind of diabolical patronage. Indeed it has been said that the name of his calling derives from a supposed element of 'Black Art'.

Legendary too, but only in the figurative sense, are the extraordinary kayak descents of the Cwm Llan cataracts made by instructors from the Plas y Brenin Activities Centre at Capel Curig.

Legend apart, Nantgwynant has seen many incursions, Celts from Europe and from Ireland, Romans whose writ did not always run, assorted Germanic tribes and finally the Normans. The latter being the first to make an enduring occupation, although at a budget-crippling expenditure on castles. Landowners have come and gone, exploiters have come and gone, trippers and excursionists come and go, but none have nor ever can impinge for long on this place.

GLASLYN
3
GIANTS AND DRAGONS

As the river approaches Llyn Dinas it shrugs off the sordid search for ores and rocks, salubriously gliding between the loom of Snowdon and the pawn-like peaks that squire the Knight-on-Horseback Cnicht.

The lake itself is not the largest, not the highest nor the deepest, in fact on paper were it not for the suicidal tendencies of its trout when sun and wind, time and season are in harmony, it would be a very average lake indeed. Speeding motorists give it scarcely a glance, conscious that it is a mere puddle compared with Tegid or Trawsfynydd. It lacks the gravitas of Ogwen; the smoulder of Idwal, the sweep of Mymbyr, yet taken as a pair with Llyn Gwynant, it lifts this valley from the ordinary to the sublime.

These lakes provided, and as far as I am aware still provide, excellent lairs for the Tylwyth Teg. In the hills they derive summer shade from fern and winter shelter from heather and gorse, but in these lowland parts their abode of choice is a lake-edge overhang.

There are those who say that since no one has seen sign or sight of them, the Tylwyth Teg do not exist. However absence of evidence is not evidence of absence, so prudence must dictate that those living near lakes such as these should keep a clean house and leave out some morsel of butter or cheese at night, since a nocturnal visit to a clean house providing a modicum of refreshment will be rewarded by a silver coin. On the other hand a dirty house with no sustenance can result in one's cows and nanny goats being sucked dry. Indeed it is said that in cases of extreme domestic neglect, a baby might be snatched and a monstrous offspring substituted.

The valley has not always been tranquil, for once Owain the Giant laid claim to it. Owain wasn't much of a giant, not in the same league as Idris who waded the Irish Sea, but a nasty piece of work all the same. Fortunately Emrys, who lived on the opposite side of the river was able to slay Owain in an epic fight.

There are those that would have us believe that the tale of Owain is merely an allegory for an Irish incursion. Alternatively Owain may have been a man on the make who, in the economic confusion that followed the Roman withdrawal, unwisely tried to muscle in on Emrys' territory. Anyway whoever he was or was not, his grave complete with marker stone is plain for all to see at the lower end of Llyn Dinas. Since Owain's shade allegedly still bestrides the valley seeking rest, to be on the safe side sculptor Dominic Clare has provided a giant-size chair high above Dinas Emrys. To avoid accusations of over-favouring the oversized, Brian and Lynne Denman have placed a more conventionally dimensioned seat overlooking Llyn Gwynant.

Now Emrys as his official name Aurelius Aurelianus indicates was a Romanised Briton. His colloquial name was Emrys Wledig a person of considerable influence, or in modern terms a 'Mr. Big'. His residence was atop the wooded knoll we call Dinas Emrys, an Iron Age site fortified by Vortigern, the de facto ruler of southern Britain during the second quarter of the 5th century.

It must be remembered that the departure of the Romans in 410 was not a single event accompanied by drums, bugles and flag lowering, but a gradual thinning of garrisons over many decades, leaving power vacua that local opportunists were quick to fill. People feared a Roman reconquest, visualising an avenging cohort lurking round every corner, in addition the Pictish hordes finding the forts of Hadrian's Wall unmanned poured south in great numbers. Thus anyone who promised to repel returning Romans and pillaging Picts could be sure of popular support giving chancers like Vortigern the opportunity to seize power. Vortigern having most unwisely employed the Saxons Hengist and Horsa to fight off the Picts, the latter eventually caught up with him, giving Emrys the opportunity to take possession of Vortigern's Welsh hideaway.

Quite who Emrys was is obscure, for despite the Welsh calling the Dark Ages, the Age of Saints, much of Wales' post-Roman period is stubbornly stygian.

Emrys seems to have been associated with Merlin [Myrddin Emrys] the magician from Caer Myrddin [Carmarthen] and they may even have been one and the same person, reputedly connected by marriage to the Emperor Constantine III. Contemporary masonry unearthed at Dinas Emrys has yielded pottery bearing the Chi-Rho symbol, confirming occupation by a Christian, which Vortigern was not, but Emrys with these imperial connections would have been.

Dinas Emrys remained a fortified site in Norman times but long before Vortigern's days it had been the lair of a red dragon. Threatened with eviction by a white dragon (Saxon invaders?) the red dragon fought with tooth, claw and of course fire, until the white dragon ran away with its tail between its legs, that given the spiky nature of a dragon's tail must have been an unpleasant experience.

Although the entrance to its lair has been lost, the red dragon apparently still lurks there, its fire-breathing mechanism ticking over in stand-by mode. Its rumble can be clearly heard by anyone blessed with sufficient aural acuity.

However it is the industrial aspect that has left more obvious remains. Close by the road is the Sygun mine, larger than other copper mines in the district, it was run in conjunction with the Hafod y Llan

copper mine and the Hafod y Llan slate quarry. Amalgamation can increase profits, but in this case served mainly to increase losses.

Sygun had its best days in the 1890s exploiting the Elmore flotation method of separation. Plant capable of processing 100 tons of ore per day gave it nearly as much capacity as all the other nearby mines combined. Despite this new technology that was rapidly applied worldwide, work had ceased by 1907.

The remains of the mine stand out from the crowd by being perched on a rocky knoll. Although it is said to be reminiscent of the Saqqara 'stepped' pyramid, it was considered sufficiently oriental in aspect to be the location for filming The Inn of the Sixth Happiness.

On the north slopes beyond Dinas Emrys was another copper mine Hafod y Porth; spread seemingly willy-nilly it was worked from the mid 18th century. Its water-powered stamps and rolls were sold off in 1845 so that when some 20 years later it was worked on a small scale with Sygun and Hafod y Llan, such ore as was produced was hauled across the mountainside to the Hafod y Llan mill. For much of the rest of the 19th century it was the subject of financial shenanigans during which time some zinc was also raised.

The ruins of Hafod y Porth mine lie within the range of the Snowdon goats, not collie-dog sized domestic animals but beasts able to eyeball a pony. The billys roam retinued by perhaps half a dozen acolytic nannies with kids to heel. If approached, they do not run away but stare with the sort of distain that Gulliver's Houyhnhnms might have reserved for a Yahoo, then having displayed their contempt they just vanish. If horns like yard-long twin antennae are spotted behind a crest, approach will reveal nothing but empty landscape. They are sometimes likened to unicorns, as gentle, ephemeral creatures, but there is nothing gentle about two mature billys locking horns in an ascendancy dispute. Nor is there anything ephemeral about an extended family's depredations in a tree plantation.

Hard by such woodlands where lurk the even more elusive but less destructive badgers and otters is the old mansion, Craflyn Hall. Once home to the influential Parry family, it is now an important National Trust hub for countryside management and a visitor centre providing a 'base camp' for walkers and climbers. Inside is a notable panoramic mural by local artist, Jenny Watts.

GLASLYN
4
BEDDGELERT

At Beddgelert, the Glaslyn confluences with the Afon Colwyn forming a veritable Clapham Junction of waters. The Colwyn is much augmented by several streams such as the Mellionen whose now wooded cwm was once well populated. It had a slate quarry which for much of the 19th century was the subject of some unsuccessful working but much successful speculation. The Afon Cloch that also fed the Colwyn, again had a slate quarry that enjoyed, if that is the word, some limited success. The Colwyn's main contributor is Afon Hafod Ruffydd that flows across an extensive hill farm of that name from the little-visited Llyn Llywelyn that, according to legend, is the footprint of a huge giant. Although this stream is usually just a brook, it swells in bad weather and incautious crossing can bring tragedy. The drowning in it of a much-respected Wise Woman [midwife] in the

early 19th century is still spoken of. Close to where this stream joins it, the Colwyn flows between two rocks into a pool rather grandly named Llyn Nâd y Forwyn *'lake of the maiden's cry'* so named from the time when a young girl was drowned in it by her swain when she refused his lustful advances, resulting in the usual stories of apparitions and of nocturnal wailings.

Besides being a conjoining of rivers, Beddgelert has since pre-history been a junction of routes, although actual roads were few and not so long ago the last wheel seen here had been attached to a Roman chariot. Even in the late 18th century a carriage in Beddgelert would have caused a stampede of sightseers. As the summertime traffic jams testify, this one-time dearth of traffic has been more than rectified. There have been many schemes to run rails through Beddgelert to service the industries of Nantgwynant, with land being bought and even earthworks constructed. In the 1870s, when the mineral and industrial prospects of the area were being described in terms that today would have courted prosecution under the Trades Descriptions Act, every offer was accompanied by an assurance that rail connection was imminent. Despite all the mineral occurrences being small and disparate and mostly not of the best quality, the whole area oozed confidence that widespread occurrences of copper and slate would make a bonanza inevitable.

The grandly named 'General Undertaking of the North Wales Narrow Gauge Railways' published plans in the 1870s to reach Beddgelert from Caernarfon and sweep on to Porthmadog, with a branch from Beddgelert along Nantgwynant to Capel Curig, Betws-y-coed and Corwen. In fact it, as one might say, 'ran out of steam' on the barren wastes of Rhyd-ddu.

At the beginning of the 20th century the Portmadog, Beddgelert and Rhyd-ddu Railway was claiming to be a precursor of a necklace of electric lines that would encircle Snowdonia powered by the hydro generators of Cwm Dyli. Unfortunately it didn't quite work out. It languished with tunnels bored and cuttings cut, with a bridge (that still spans the road at Beddgelert) unused, the haunches of a river crossing and standing solitary in a field, the ramparts of an accommodation underpass in an embankment that was never

embanked. The sole tangible asset for this nascent electric railway was one steam locomotive! This engine the Russell is still in use at Porthmadog on the Welsh Highland Railway

It would be the 1920s before Beddgelert even heard an engine's whistle, by which time goods were going by lorry and passengers by bus. Forestry roads define the direct course of the electric lines' earthworks down the Colwyn valley from Pitts Head; earthworks that the steam line (and its 21st century reincarnation) had to eschew in favour of more sinuous routes to keep the gradient profile within steam capabilities.

However, Beddgelert *'Gelert's grave'* is inextricably associated with the legend of Gelert the faithful hound of the Great Prince Llywelyn. While the Prince went out hunting, he set the dog to guard his infant son. On his return, finding the boy missing and the dog's jaws dripping with blood he, with one angry lunge of his sword, slew the dog. Attracted by a whimper, he discovered the baby unharmed beneath a blanket. Outside was the corpse of a savaged wolf, clearly killed by Gelert defending his charge.

Central to the village and the legend, is the Goat Hotel. Not the excellent present day establishment with its 'Royal' prefix but its 18th century predecessor. Like hostelries at that time it lacked not just mod cons, but any kind of cons at all and a drunken landlord serving uneatable fare was to be expected. The weary guest might well find himself sharing a room or even a bed with a fellow traveller, or perhaps the Ostler or the Boots, each redolent of his trade. Rats (and with luck cats and dogs to catch them) coursing around the bedroom would be so commonplace as to escape mention, but what famed the old Goat throughout the land was the number and ferocity of its fleas. One did not dare kill a flea, since its death would be avenged by a voracious invasion of its relatives.

It was said to be preferable to sleep with a goat than at the Goat. That peripatetic cleric, the Rev. Bingley on his Cymric Journey, when rating hotels in order of awfulness seems to have taken the Goat as his nadir.

When the hotel was rebuilt in the early 19th century to cope with the turnpike traffic, the proprietor realised that some signal attraction was needed to overcome its predecessor's stigma. With flair worthy of Madison Avenue, he hijacked the Gelert legend, claiming that the Bedd [grave] referred to the hound's last resting place and not to that of Saint Celert from whom the name actually derives. To prove it, he built a 'grave' that has been a place of pilgrimage for the better part of two centuries. The 'grave' has been augmented in the ruins of Beudy Buarth Gwyn farm by a bronze statue of 'Gelert' by Cardiff based sculptor Rowleigh Clay. This statute is of such realism that passing dogs pause to sniff its nether regions. The area and its woodlands, the haunt of polecats and

reputedly pine martens is enhanced artistically by Dominic Clare's wooden sculptures and practically by his and Iona McClaggan's gates. In the woods are stoats, weasels and small rodents, prey to ravens and other avian predators who are no longer imperilled by gamekeepers.

Long before Beddgelert became industrially aspirational and a landlord's gimmick, it had been an important religious settlement. Following the disappearance of the Romans there were some invasions, but unusually for somewhere then so close to navigable water, it saw nothing of the Vikings who presumably never risked the rain of rocks that would have awaited them in the Aberglaslyn Gorge. Thus, until the coming of the Normans in the late 11th century, the 'Age of Saints' could develop for some 600 years free from heathen incursions. The present St Mary's church probably marks the site of the first monastic settlement, the 5th century foundation associated with St Celert.

This religious settlement was revived as an Augustinian priory in the early 12th century. Despite the dominance of Welsh religious (and economic) life by the great Cistercian abbeys, generous patronage was secured from princes such as Llywelyn ap Iorwerth, with numerous grants of land. The priory was a major influence on the area, hence following fire damage in 1283, in an unusually display of open-handedness, Edward I paid for repairs to keep it 'On side'. The priory was dissolved in the 16th century, but its influence on land ownership was still being felt in the 19th century.

It has been claimed that the priory was the burial place of Owain Glyndŵr, whose last fugitive days were allegedly spent in a cave high on Moel Hebog.

Following successive careers as a centre of religion, legend and of industry, Beddgelert boosted by several active voluntary bodies flourishes as never before as a caterer to tourists. A chapel, sadly like so many, now redundant has been most sympathetically converted into a Visitor Centre.

GLASLYN
5
ABERGLASLYN & SECRET VALLEYS

An 18th century visitor wrote of the Aberglaslyn gorge –

How shall I express my feelings! The dark tremendous precipice. The rapid river roaring over disjointed rock, black caverns and issuing cataracts, all serve to make this the noblest specimen of the Finely Horrid the eye can possibly behold: the poet has not described nor the painter pictured so gloomy a retreat, 'tis the last Approach to the mansion of Pluto through the regions of despair'.

Nowadays visitors are less negative. Aberglaslyn's views challenge both artists and photographers, while in its pools the salmon challenge anglers, but the greatest challenge is that of the cataracts to canoeists, varying from the tyro's Grade II to the expert's Grade V. Despite the tunnels of the Welsh Highland Railway being closed to them, walkers eagerly make their way along

its banks savouring both its beauty and its flora.

Aberglaslyn Hall is now an outdoor pursuits centre; but still in private occupation is nearby Dôl Friog, a house that in 1878 the great diva Adelina Patti considered buying. Her eventual choice of Craig y Nos in southern Wales was undoubtedly welcomed hereabouts since she was living in 'notorious sin' with husband-to-be, Ernesto Nicholini, while still married to the Marquis de Caux (what else could one expect from performers and foreign ones at that?).

Long before visitors abounded, and divas dithered, even before there was a proper road, mining adventurers were busy in the gorge. From mines that are now the haunts of bats, copper ores were pannier-donkeyed to the little port of Aber that in pre-Porthmadog Cob times nestled close below

the bridge. Also just below the bridge was the cave where the crews of Swansea ore vessels hid their contraband.

As regards Pont Aberglaslyn itself, it appears that the local people urgently needed such a facility but lacked both the wherewithal and the skills for such a tricky structure. Apparently a pact was made with the devil who agreed to span the gorge in return for the soul of the first user. The bridge appeared in a flash and immediately a man volunteered to cross, but his nerve failed halfway, and he stopped and retraced his steps but his dog carried on, so the devil had to be content with the soul of the dog.

Not a sheep's leap from Pont Aberglaslyn, the little Bychan stream has in the course of a million years created a valley where the perfumes of the flora conspire to complement the

vistas, the pungency of the wild garlic being deferentially muted. Even the alien cypress trees, absconders from some exotic garden, merge into the landscape.

The sheep tiptoe, chewing in refined silence, only the almost inaudible scuttle of a startled stoat impinges upon the tranquillity. Here the sound of a motor vehicle would seem as anachronistic as it would have been a thousand years ago.

This is Cwm Bychan, that provides for those prepared to tread its gentle ascent on foot-comforting sward, a view of startling richness.

At the entrance to the valley the arch of the Welsh Highland Railway that was to have carried its cuprous bounties, and the buddles and the processing plant bases of the reckless 1920s investment, remind one of its industrial past. Nearby at the old sheep-dip pool, there is a curious circular iron cage that more mischievous guides will describe as an updated ducking stool that enabled miscreants to be immersed in the stream. It was actually (stone filled) the tensioning weight for the gravity ropeway, whose four rusting towers still defy the scrap merchant's cutter to grace rather than intrude upon the scene.

Cwm Bychan mine could not be honestly described as a success, although it bumbled its way through the 19th century, with episodic claims of 'rich veins' of copper, gold and lead, until the railway's arrival spurred the largely fruitless attempts at modernisation.

Besides the ore heaps, there is an outstanding example of a dressing floor, where women and girls would hammer into manageable pieces the great hunks of ore that their men folk had hacked from the underground stopes. This division of labour kept the women from the hazards of mining but left them unprotected from the weather.

Conventional terms such as 'bucketing' and 'stair-rods' fail to convey the intensity of the Cwm Bychan rain which when impelled by winds funnelling up the cwm makes a mockery of the most impermeable of clothing. One wonders at the stamina of the 'Copper Ladies' stooping to their task, a sodden sack across their shoulders, their gloveless, frozen fingers grasping the lacerating ores, their earthy banter scarcely blunted by the relentless rain beating on their saturated backs.

At the crest was the horse-whim of Llwyndu copper mine that wound ore from the depths tp send to Mr Hendry Bath's Swansea Landore Copper Works. But here, among the mining waste, barren screes and goat-defeating gorse is revealed with explosive suddenness and eye-stunning panorama, a God's eye view of the lushness of Nantgwynant far below.

The Nanmor valley, a little distance off, is something of a contrast. Following a geological fault-line it forms a groove through the foothills of the Cnichtian block. Its road, a tight squeeze for a broad-shouldered cyclist, follows the stream forming a back lane, a sort of tradesman's entrance for the main street of Nantgwynant.

Sylvan today, there were once almost half a dozen slate workings, including Berth Lwyd, where a Victorian slate quarry was dug in the back garden of a Tudor house that following decades of dereliction, has been lovingly restored.

Hard by Berth Lwyd, where the road bridges the river, is a level patch of ground, the *Clwt Powlio* 'hurling patch' where some arcane precursor of football was played, allegedly with a stone 'ball' (!)

Delighting the eye to the southeast are streams and waterfalls that nourish the river with tinkling cataracts, deriving their sustenance from almost countless lakes. Presiding over these lakes is Llyn yr Adar whose name, the *'lake of birds'* is now largely justified by the black-headed gulls that squat in the tiny islet noisily discussing the brown trout. A stream

draining it hesitates uncertainly before careering down into Llyn Llagi, a turgid, cliff-dominated lake whose piscatorial potential was first recognised by James Spooner, the engineer of the Ffestiniog Railway.

Perhaps more exciting is Llyn Arddu, half hidden among the rocky outcrops. Legend has it that a hobgoblin lurks in its depths, but faintly more factual is the nearby Ogof y Lleidr *'robber's cave'*, the lair of a robber, whose depredations were stopped when a shepherd caught him asleep and dispatched him with his own sword. Confusingly, claim to this legend is also laid by an adjacent lake that supports its bid with the name Llyn yr Ogof *'lake of the cave'* and traces of a vestigial cavern.

Close by are the twin lakes of Cerrig y Myllt *'rock of the wethers'* and nearby is Bwlch y 'Batel *'battle pass'*, the site of a battle during the Wars of the Roses, where weapons have been unearthed.

Every valley in Wales claims a poet, Nanmor claims two: Dafydd Nanmor in the 15th century who was a master of the *Cywydd* form of verse and Rhys Nanmor in the 16th century. Regrettably this poet-per-century scoring rate proved unsustainable among such a sparse population.

As well as a shortage of poets, there was a shortage of people, thus a young man might seek to avoid incestuous intermarriage by taking a bride from the Tylwyth Teg, quite an attraction since girl fairies were blessed with beauty that surpassed that of any human. Such unions could pose procreative problems since many fairy maidens were repelled by human touch and since even the most innocent pre-nuptial contact would be intolerable, espousal was a gamble. Should the bride prove to be possessed by this unfortunate allergy, offspring would have to be magically manufactured. Such issue would have gifts of prophesy that would distinguish them from infants created by more conventional means.

GLASLYN
6
CROESOR & LLANFROTHEN

Northbound travellers who, fortified by refreshment at the Tan y Bwlch inn having climbed from the Dwyryd valley, would cross Cwm Croesor before negotiating the rocky descent to Nanmor. They would be treading footprints both of the Romans and those of Elen [Helen] of Sarn Elen fame. Here this Celtic Princess met her sons returning from battle, but they were not carrying their shields, their shields were carrying them, whereupon she cried *Croes awr yw hon i mi* [this is a bad hour for me], hence giving the name to this ancient hanging valley teetering high above the estuarial Glaslyn – according to one popular story!

The reclamation of the Glaslyn estuary enabled a less taxing route to be built, leaving Croesor's cottages and marginal farms undisturbed by passers-by and the soothsaying widow custodian of Ffynnon Elen *'Helen's well'* unpatronised.

Almost uniquely for a Welsh village it only had one chapel, two being the accepted minimum *'One to go to, the other never set foot in!'* There is (but not for much longer!) a fine school presided over for an appreciable proportion of the 20th century by headmistress Gwyneth Morgan who was held in such regard that when she retired in 2000, pupils past and present created a garden surrounded by slate 'standing stones' recording Croesor history.

It was in the mid 19th century when the clatter of a mail coach was fading from living memory that serious slate extraction began. The quarries brought more than just incomers and jobs, they brought the Tramway with its embankments, epic inclines and monumental drum houses, one of which was made into a mini banqueting hall by Clough Williams-Ellis the be-breeched creator of Portmeirion.

There was one big house, Parc, a fine Tudor dwelling that still stands having been originally built for the Anwyliaid, a numerous family, influential throughout Meirionnydd. An upgrading and extension of the access to this house became the present road to Croesor from Garreg.

The appellation Parc was adopted by a quarry that, under the guidance of the great Moses Kellow, became one of the most innovative slate undertakings in Wales; famed for its 'Parcro Patent Ridging' that can still be seen on the manager's house. (Kellow's own home stands at the head of the valley dominating the area just as he himself did.)

Even more famed than Kellow was his clerk, Bob Owen. Born at Llanfrothen in 1885, he was a farm worker before joining the Parc and Croesor Slate Quarry Company at their Porthmadog office. When he was in his mid-forties the quarries closed and for a time he worked as a council clerk, but in later life devoted himself to more cerebral activities as a lecturer with the Workers' Education Association and an historian and genealogist with a special interest in the Quakers. His book-crammed, chapel-adjacent home, Ael y Bryn, was visited by ancestor-seekers from all over the world. He was awarded an MA and created an OBE, and undoubtedly served as an example to those who have since abandoned modest occupations to achieve academic accolades.

The Parc road to Croesor leaves Garreg Llanfrothen at the Brondanw Arms opposite which is a fanciful gatehouse, a creation of the equally fanciful Clough Williams-Ellis. His house, Plas Brondanw, that he was forced to rebuild after a disastrous fire that would have daunted a lesser man, is just up the hill. It is half hidden, but everywhere around Garreg, from the fine roadside monument to the tiniest of touches unexpectedly encountered at every turn, are quirky reminders that we are in the land of Clough.

It is difficult to realise that where Garreg church now stands was once under water and that the Brondanw Arms was at a shipping point and ferry terminal from whence travellers to Garndolbenmaen and beyond could fortify themselves for the rigours and perils of the crossing to Pren-teg.

Whilst Garreg Llanfrothen is a thriving settlement, Llanfrothen itself, where once lead, copper and slate were won, is now a mere vestigial hamlet. Its road once an important route is now a little-used and ill-maintained lane. Its church, where spring tides once advanced up its sloping aisle and was often best reached by boat, is now semi-abandoned. Yet the now overgrown churchyard once shaped world events.

In 1916 the Prime Minister was the ailing Asquith. It is generally accepted that had he remained in office, the Great War could well have been lost, had a less than exceptional man replaced Asquith it could not have been won.

That exceptional replacement was David Lloyd George. Although latterly lampooned for his simplistic approach to certain aspects of accepted morality, Ll. G's manifest abilities enabled him to effortlessly vault from the backbenches to the Dispatch Box. However, at that time for a fatherless boy from an obscure village in remotest Wales to become a Member of Parliament, would have seemed impossible. Indeed it might well have been had it not been for the Llanfrothen Burial Case.

In these ecumenical days it is difficult to realise the strength of inter-denominational ill feeling that once existed in Wales.

For much of the 19th century, to match the population explosion that accompanied Wales becoming the first industrialised nation on earth, a place of worship opened every eight days. Most of these were not churches but non-conformist chapels. The church-going, Tory-voting landlords felt swamped by this tidal wave of Baptists Wesleyans, Presbyterians and Congregationalists (to name only the 'leading brands' of dissent). These chapelgoers included many Liberal-leaning industrialists happy to finance their chapels, but resentful of the Tithe system that forced them to also support the churches and clergy.

In 1888 Robert Roberts, a retired Croesor quarryman, died. He had expressed a wish to be buried by his chapel minister next to his daughter, a churchwoman who had been buried at her parish church, (old) Llanfrothen. Although every parish resident had a legal right to be buried in a churchyard, accompanied by the rites of any denomination, the vicar would have none of it.

Folklore has it that the funeral procession was led by Lloyd George, who finding the

church gate secured, broke the chain with his bare hands; the truth is less dramatic. The mourners frustrated by a chained gate, returned next day with tools. Supported by a number of influential Liberal stalwarts, they forced the gate enabling a chapel minister to carry out the committal and interment.

The vicar went to law alleging trespass and the defendants engaged Lloyd George, then a young solicitor who had recently established a law practice in Llanystumdwy in a room in his shoemaker uncle's cottage. The vicar acknowledged the right of dissenters to conduct their own burials in churchyards, but argued that this burial did not take place in the 'official' churchyard, but in an annexe bequeathed to the church for burial purposes (the grave can be seen in what is clearly an extension).

Lloyd George lost the case, unkind people say deliberately. If this is true then it was a wise move, since backed by funds supplied by wealthy Liberal non-conformists, an appeal could be lodged.

The appeal was held in London and was reported in the national press, thus giving the appellants a stage on which to attack the Church, the Tories and the landowners.

Some of these appellants were Blaenau Ffestiniog slate entrepreneurs who were delighted to have an opportunity to give some stick to the big Caernarfon quarry owners who were firmly in the Tory/Church camp.

The appeal court ruled that the annexe was part of the churchyard vindicating the dissenters' actions, thus converting a young lawyer from the darkest, and most unpronounceable depths of Wales into a national hero. Within two years he was in Parliament.

The gate is still there (minus the broken chain!) as is the church that has proved more durable than its Garreg-Llanfrothen successor, which has needed extensive repairs.

GLASLYN
7
PREN-TEG & TREMADOG

According to legend, Pren-teg is where Prince Madog, son of Owain Gwynedd sailed west to anticipate Columbus by three centuries and to found a tribe of Welsh speaking Native Americans. Once a shipyard and port it served the Pennant valley, shipping the output and housing the men of several slate quarries. Now land-locked, thanks to the Prince's near-namesake W.A. Madocks'

draining of Traeth Mawr, Pren-teg finds fresh fame thanks to the ospreys nesting at nearby Pont Croesor. This area has long acted as a motel for migratory birds, not always welcome when the birds are large and numerous, but when in 2005 a pair of ospreys was seen to be not resting but nesting, it created an ornithological sensation. Thanks to the vigilance and enterprise of the RSPB and many volunteers they have annually returned creating a mini-industry.

This reclamation by Madocks was spurred by the Anglo-Irish Act of Union of 1800, which united the two great financial centres of London and Dublin, giving rise to a need for fast communication between them. Although Telford with his great London-Holyhead road would shortly prove them wrong, many declared the Menai Strait unbridgeable, thus Porth

Dinllaen in Llŷn was identified as a site for a packet-port.

Madocks having already successfully revived a 17th century scheme to drain land where Tremadog now stands commenced in 1808 to build a great embankment across the Glaslyn estuary. This would not only create hundreds of acres of dry land, but also provide a roadway (on which he could charge a toll!) that would be part of a new coach road to Porth Dinllaen.

Where the road across the newly reclaimed ground from the Cob embankment met the Penmorfa-Pont Aberglaslyn road adjacent to houses already built, he laid out a fine square in Regency style. Against the backdrop of the cliffs, a quite magnificent Town Hall was built, not the modern abode of clerks and functionaries, but a proper Town Hall where anything from a market to a masked ball might be held. Next-door he built a hotel that like the new town, bore a Gallic version of his name, furnished and fitted to a standard appropriate to the expected travelling clientele – the Jet Set of their day. A door afforded direct connection from the first floor of the hotel to the upper floor of the Town Hall, thus benighted couples seeking to pass the evening in merry minuet might pass directly from their boudoirs to the ballroom, the wives' crinolines unsullied by the elements.

Later this door had to be sealed since to have bedrooms so readily accessible from a dance floor was considered liable to encourage behaviour entirely inappropriate to as respectable an establishment as the Royal Madoc Arms.

Spiritual requirements were catered for by St Mary's church (now sensitively converted into offices). Perched on a rock, it was a very early example of Gothic revival. The spire is rendered in Parker's Roman Cement, but sadly the specially cast iron window frames have succumbed to the saline environment. The fine arched gateway of Coade Stone was shipped in "Self Assembly" kit form from London. Both Coade's and Parker's products were highly innovative at the time as was the concept of "Prefab" construction.

Having built an English church, a religious even-handedness was displayed by building Peniel, a Welsh Presbyterian chapel whose Greek portico added in the 1840s has flatteringly been widely copied.

A 'Manufactory' where wool was carded and spun ensured that the Devil did not find work for idle hands. The adjoining, particularly fine five-storey 60-loom weaving shed, probably the first factory of its kind in Wales, was painted an

olive green to merge in with the scenery, anticipating military camouflage by a century. Unfortunately this 'Sheep's back to wearer's back' enterprise was beset by legal disputes and wild accusations that it was supplying broadcloth to Napoleon's armies, but it managed to survive to supply uniforms for the British troops in the Crimea. The site and buildings have been put to a number of subsequent uses including a redolently regrettable tannery.

Tremadog grew apace, acquiring that sine-que-non of early 19th century civic status, a canal. It did serve to bring in supplies and it has been asserted that a trans-Atlantic voyage started from its now lost basin. The canal still holds water, which many of its grander contemporaries do not. A tramway from an ironstone mine ran along its bank, the formation of this short-lived line being utilised by the Gorseddau slate railway in its several gauges and guises. Nowadays as a footpath and cycle track it probably carries more traffic than ever.

By the 1820s the Penmorfa market had been moved to Tremadog which was said to have - *Eighty to a hundred houses and a great number of good shops*, the town's success being ascribed to its having been planned by - *A person of cultivated mind, of improved tastes and superior knowledge.*

Unfortunately things had not quite turned out as expected, Port Dinllaen never happened, the Cob was breached in 1812 only months after completion and despite scores of horses, carts and men being generously loaned, the cost of repairs ruined Madocks.

The rich alluvial soil re-claimed by Madocks' efforts unlocked a whole new agricultural aspect to those farming it. Whilst much was too saline for crops most made good gradientless grazing. Heather did not have to be shunned nor the good soil of gorse or better still bracken sought on steep rocky hillsides in a search for sheep sustenance. Tŷ Newydd Morfa (near the osprey nest observation site) was one such farm, but apparently the cows' milk yield proved most disappointing. After local advice was unavailing, help was sought from Bela Fawr, a mystic lady from Denbigh. Taking her gun, she hid overnight in a holly bush and just before dawn caught a hare suckling the cows. She shot the creature but her silver bullet merely grazed it. Following the trail of blood to Pant y Wrach on the edge of the estuary, she found an old woman, Cadi'r Wrach, with blood at her feet. Bela decided that the old woman has been frightened enough and predicted, correctly, that Tŷ Newydd's cattle would not be molested again.

All Tremadog's factories and mills were powered from Llyn Cwm Bach. Near this part-artificial lake a quarry was established during the post-WW1 slate boom, the first new slate opening for several decades and the first in modern times to be sited without regard to waterpower or rail access. Sadly this enterprise, so very much in keeping with the earlier innovativeness of Madocks, was a failure.

Happily, an exact replica has

replaced the famous street-corner Chemist's slate sign that was stolen in the 1990s and in Church Street a plaque marks the birthplace of Tremadog's most famous son T. E. Lawrence, the enigmatic 'Lawrence of Arabia'. Regrettably the room in which he was born now serves as a toilet in the Snowdon Lodge hostel.

On the steep wooded hinterland behind the town is Tan yr Allt the magnificently verandaed home that William Madocks rebuilt to his own design, commanding (as house agents put it) the finest maritime view in Wales. Or at least it did until Madocks himself marred the vista with his reclamation scheme! Whilst Madocks' attributes were manifold, he did have one shortcoming – an admiration for the poet Percy Bysshe Shelley, whose views on politics and other matters were widely controversial. When the 20-year-old Shelley said in 1812 that the next year he would come into a fortune which he would use to bail out the creditor-beset Madocks, the latter lent him the house, ostensibly so that he might establish some kind of co-operative community. One night the household was wakened by a pistol shot. Shelley displaying a torn nightgown alleged that an intruder had made an attempt on his life and insisted that a horse be saddled so he could instantly depart. He did so, ending up in Ireland, his community unestablished, and the local tradesmen unpaid.

J. W. Greaves the great Blaenau Ffestiniog slate proprietor moved into Tan yr Allt from more modest adjoining premises in the 1840s when his Llechwedd quarry began to make serious money. Prior to that the sett had proved barren, leaving Greaves effectively penniless. A group of his men agreed to work on without pay until the powder and so on was used up. When supplies were on the point of exhaustion, Greaves was roused in the night by a breathless rider beating on his door to announce that the riches of the Meirionnydd Old Vein had been struck. It is said that thereafter the Greaves family have seen that those men and their descendants, were never in want.

To the regret of some, Greaves' extension and bay windows have marred the symmetry of Madocks' design. Greaves family members sporadically occupied the house until it became a school in 1985. It is recorded that in the 1900s this residence, modest by gentry standards, had 3 maids a cook and 2 gardeners as well as a

chauffeur to manage the new-fangled motorcar. It is now a splendid hotel.

Larger than Tan yr Allt is Wern, a fine mansion now a care home but once occupied by R.M. Greaves the talented marine engineer son of J.W. (and adviser to the Japanese navy!), whose inventiveness helped to keep Llechwedd in the forefront of innovation. He was renowned for the fostering of music and for entertaining the great and the good, including such 'A listers' as the Queen of Romania. A house party once included Lord Baden-Powell who pitched his tent on the east lawn.

Before Greaves' time Wern was the home of Nathaniel Matthew, a substantial but largely unsung Blaenau quarry proprietor whose influence on Blaenau and Porthmadog was decisive. In 1842, hearing of a great fire in Hamburg he immediately travelled there, arriving almost before the blaze was extinguished, to take orders for the re-building. This proved to be the start of the great Baltic trade that contributed so much to the prosperity of Porthmadog and Blaenau.

Just along the Beddgelert Road is Craig Bwlch y Moch a cliff popular with climbers because it is so readily accessible, has year-round potential and offers routes of varying difficulty. Climbers can be refreshed, regaled and advised at the adjacent café by proprietor Eric Jones, the first Briton to solo the north wall of the Eiger.

Further along is Portreuddyn a small estate where vernacular slate quarrying was carried out close to what had been the water's edge. Despite Madocks' reclamation denying it this shipping facility, the quarry quietly survived to become an early user of steam power.

GLASLYN
8
PORTHMADOG

Traditionally, Porthmadog and its Tre'r Gest hinterland are epicentred neither at the harbour nor the town but at Ynyscynhaearn whose parish stretched from Cricieth to the Glaslyn, its acreage outnumbering its headcount a dozen fold. The little church of St Cynhaearn and the adjacent Ystumllyn house represented a substantial proportion of its built environment.

The churchyard, sentinelled by a constabulary of crows, affords safe and final anchorage for captains and crewmen, and rest for wives who waited and watched so often in vain for a sail to break the far horizon. Here too, silently incised in slate, is the harp that marks the grave of Dafydd y Garreg Wen whose *Rising of the Lark* inspired Elgar's *Nimrod* that resounds around the world from the Cenotaph each Remembrance Sunday.

The building of Tremadog and the prospect of the passage of English sophisticates must have been something of a culture shock in this ocean of tranquillity, but that was as nothing compared with the almost magical manifestation of Porthmadog.

This sort of Tremadog-on-sea was made possible by the fortuitous silting and scour of the Glaslyn River caused by Madocks' Cob producing the nucleus of a shipping point. This development which was not, in the modern argot, so much 'Green Field' as 'Blue Water', leaped from nothing to being the busiest non-coal port in Wales in little more than a generation.

By 1825 a wharf was built (near the present Ffestiniog Railway station) enabling Blaenau Ffestiniog slate, barged down the Dwyryd that hitherto had been trans-shipped at sea, to be landed and re-shipped at a quayside. In a further fortuitous coincidence, ballast dumped by boats arriving unladen to take slate on board, made an island that virtually created a harbour.

As for the Cob, although posh passengers and vital dispatches never thundered along it four-in-hand to Ireland, it provided in 1836, a bed for that doyen of the tracks, the Ffestiniog Railway

Thus virtually accidentally, a town not so much grew up, as 'Hit the ground running', to function as a port and support centre for Blaenau Ffestiniog. Virtually every technical, professional,

commercial, engineering and maritime service that Blaenau required came to be based here. Thus Porthmadog and Blaenau formed two mutually dependent halves of one industrial complex, united by the Ffestiniog Railway lifeline.

Although, as a totally new town every inhabitant was an incomer, it seems to have been a cohesive community from its earliest days, largely due to the influence of the nonconformist chapels. The first settlers could attend Peniel at Tremadog, but in 1826, less than a year after the first wharf opened, Salem (Congregationalist) was established at Porthmadog itself. Over the next couple of decades chapels appeared catering for every denominational nuance as well as both Welsh and English linguistic requirements. These chapels were not just for Sundays, but were daily centres for social, educational and almost every other purpose. It would not have been unusual for a person to attend chapel every evening of the week for one reason or another.

Chapels were paid for by ordinary folk, the churches by the landowners. Since the town had no landowner to build a church (there had not been any land to own!) the Church of England (as it then was) was unrepresented among the sectarian structures. Those who wished to pray where the bosses prayed had to make do with St Mary's at Tremadog. It was 1884, by which time there was an influential middle-class of captains, shipping agents, lawyers and quarry officials, before Porthmadog had its own church (St John's) and became a full parish in its own right.

Most unusually for a maritime town, Porthmadog had few public houses and no brothels. This was attributed to the all-pervading influence of the chapels but it was more likely to have been due to the fact that most vessels using the port were locally manned. Thus a paid-off seaman would be dispossessed of his voyage-pay by no harlot, varlet or victualler, but by a quayside-waiting, umbrella-brandishing wife.

The nucleus of the town was the main coach road (which, with Porth Dinllaen never happening, might have been called the coach-less road!). Originally somewhat sinuous, it was disciplined in 1841 to run straight from the Cob skirting the docks, warehouses, chandleries and ranks of shipyards and when it seemed to be aiming for Ynyscynhaearn and Cricieth, it did a guardsman's sharp right-wheel towards Tremadog. The triangle in the crook of this elbow was laid out in a gridiron pattern of residential terraces; the hypotenuse of this triangle defined by the canal and the Croesor/Gorseddau tramways formed an axis of industry. Where the latter joined the Ffestiniog

Railway near its present terminus, were the quarry offices and the port officials, and the two main foundries, the Glaslyn and the Britannia that together catered for every sort of casting or ironwork that the quarries, the railways or the ships might require. Sadly all trace of both these famed establishments have vanished; the Glaslyn transmogrified into a Tax Office, the Britannia into a Co-op Supermarket (that has in its turn vanished). Nearby there is little trace of the great manufacturing merchants such as Davies Bros and Richard Williams who could bankroll or bankrupt any quarry company with equal ease.

During the middle years of the 19th century ever increasing amounts of slate arrived at the port carried by three separate narrow-gauge railways. Whilst the Croesor's contribution was modest and the Gorseddau's merely token, that of the Ffestiniog Railway most certainly was neither. Originally FR trains of scores of gravity-impelled wagons thundered down from Blaenau's more than a dozen quarries, the several hundred wheels banshee-screaming on the curves. Clinging as if his life depended on it (which it did!) was the brakeman striving to control this snaking juggernaut. The last vehicle was a dandy-car carrying a bemused horse that would draw the train across the Cob

and later return the empties to Blaenau. This clanking, Isaac Newton-dependent anachronism was replaced in 1863 by the present steam layout. Slate tonnages doubled, redoubled then doubled again, in an avalanche that all but overwhelmed the port.

The Cambrian main line railway was able to tap into Croesor traffic via its Beddgelert siding, a stub of the Beddgelert Railway-that-never-was, and FR traffic could also reach the Cambrian by surreptitious shuntings along the Croesor metals. However, the

real opportunity for the railway to rob the docks came with the opening of the Minffordd depot. This immediately began to siphon off big tonnages, becoming the busiest depot in the world devoted to interchanging narrow gauge with standard gauge freight traffic. With slate outputs expanding so rapidly, it scarcely dented Porthmadog harbour's figures.

All this time ships were being built here and at Borth-y-Gest, and further afield at Pwllheli and elsewhere supported by timber-yards, sail makers and chandlers of every kind. Returning vessels jostled with new-built craft arriving from the boat-yards, fighting for quay space, to be loaded to the gunwales with slate for the Balkans or the Baltic, Valparaiso or Vancouver.

The ship owners were mostly men of modest means taking 64th shares of vessels, with perhaps captains, shopkeepers and professional men taking 'ounces' (16th parts), and forming mutual insurance societies to protect their investments. Aspiring master mariners were trained in schools of navigation often run by captains' widows. Some of the very earliest building societies were formed to cope with the housing needs of the burgeoning population.

In the 1880s when quarry men were being laid off in other areas, Blaenau quarries was taking them on, and in the 1890s when the rest of the industry was making a cautious recovery, Blaenau and hence Porthmadog, was forging ahead.

By that time what was not forging ahead was shipbuilding; it had become possible to buy from Canada a complete fully rigged and equipped ship for little more than the local yards would pay for their timber. Even so, such was the reputation of its 'Western Ocean Yachts' that when other ports had ceased to build, some Porthmadog slipways remained in business into the 20th century.

But foreign-built ships and iron steamers kept the wharves busy with future trade projections being extrapolated into infinity. A long-standing scheme to make the Glaslyn bridge openable, and create a quarter mile of wharf along the landward side of the Cob was revived. Sadly in the early 1900s even Blaenau's slate trade took a downturn and with the railway having an increasing share of diminishing tonnages, the new dock was not to be. The steam flour mill, one of the earliest to use steel rolls instead of millstones,

built in anticipation of wheat being directly craned from transatlantic vessels in the landward side of this great new harbour, had to be supplied by trucks running on Croesor tracks.

Now with all sea-freight long gone, Porthmadog has had to find a new role, as famously has the Ffestiniog Railway. Although it no longer crosses the Glaslyn to the quays now packed not with slates but with slate roofs, it flourishes as never before. At the other end of the town the Welsh Highland Railway occupies the track bed of the old Beddgelert siding but these rail arrangements will be changed when the WHR line comes through from Caernarfon. As it is, Porthmadog has three railway stations; more than many cities can lay claim to.

Businesses are now geared to the needs not of the voyager, but the tripper. The Town Hall has gone, but happily new uses have been found for many notable buildings such as the great steam flourmill, the premises of the great Griffith Williams School of Navigation and the fine sail loft.

The old residential streets as straight as the architect's ruler that defined them, are excitingly interspersed with little infill buildings and tiny lanes through which the night-soil man could discreetly thread his noxious cart. There are also the grander houses of the captains and professional and businessmen, although most are mid 19th century, the Regency influence of Madocks' Tremadog is strong,

Among surviving structures is the tollhouse an exceptionally complete slate-clad building that is a prime example of Parcro Patent Ridging. Also surviving nearby at the end of Madoc Street are several quarry office buildings, where pens were pushed by intellectual giants such as bibliophile and man of letters, Bob Owen and the school-master/preacher Eliseus Williams aka, Prifardd Eifion Wyn, a poet cast in the Taliesin mould.

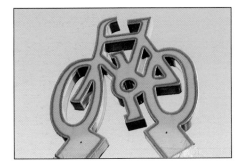

DWYRYD

Afon Dwyryd

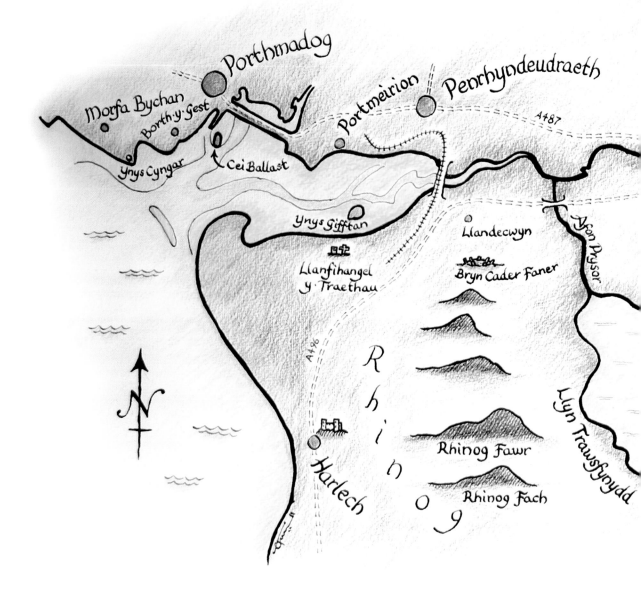

Porthmadog

Morfa Bychan

Borth-y-Gest

Ynys Cyngar

Cei Ballast

Portmeirion

Penrhyndeudraeth

A487

Afon Prysor

Ynys Gifftan

Llandecwyn

Bryn Cader Faner

Llanfihangel y Traethau

A496

Rhinog

Rhinog Fawr

Rhinog Fach

Llyn Trawsfynydd

Harlech

N

DWYRYD
9
BOWYDD & BARLWYD

These sister rivers, substantial contributors to the Dwyryd, have spectacular cascades but these are brief episodes in their life of toil for, unlike some of the other members of the Dwyryd family, these never just gave a spin to the occasional water wheel but were solid day-in-day-out workers; the power base of Blaenau Ffestiniog.

Slate quarrying requires water, lots of water, to lay the dust, to scour slurries, to cool saws and to dampen block, but at one time the need was immeasurably more. Slate quarrying is traditionally a marginal industry that so often could fall into what is now euphemistically called 'Negative Profit.' Thus in the mid 19th century, when saws, planers, dressers, pumps and hoists began to abound, energy to power them had to be cheap. The price of coal delivered to a bleak mountaintop could

be treble the pithead figure, so water became not so much the power-source of choice as the power-source of necessity. Even when the intensity of operations called for the widespread use of steam, every possible use and re-use was still made of water power.

The Bowydd drains Llyn Bowydd, an ancient lake linked to Arthurian legend, that derives it waters from countless springlets that escape from a cloying acidic peat marsh almost 1500' above sea level. It was much enlarged in the mid 19th century by a fine stone dam, as was its partner Llyn Newydd. Both have some fish and some bird life but their purpose is dedicatedly industrial.

Before the infant Bowydd could draw breath, it was elaborately leated away from its natural route to be enrolled into the service of Maenofferen slate quarry first to turn the massive mill wheel, then later to drive a hydroelectric station.

Eventually escaping from channels and culverts, the river bursts unconstrained into its own sylvan valley a stone's roll below the town of Blaenau Ffestiniog, reinforcing itself with the Afon Dubach that is fed by the almost entirely artificial Llyn Dubach. The latter's waters no longer needed by Graig Du quarry, still cascade at the Pant yr Ynn mill that Diphwys Casson built alongside its great road that enabled its slate carts to reach the turnpike at Llan Ffestiniog. Near where the Dubach joins the Bowydd is

Pont Fron Goch that was pivotal to transport for almost all early Blaenau industry.

Below Pont Fron Goch bleakness, urbanisation and industry yields to the true rurality of Cwm Bowydd. Here in pastoral surroundings river and people relax. Looking up, Blaenau Ffestiniog becomes a Tuscan hill town, a tower-less Urbino or even some say, a Jerusalem with the Bowydd its Kidron.

The Barlwyd differs from the Bowydd in that its source is not in a bog but on the clear mountainside. The twin lakes, from which the river takes its name as well as its water, were enlarged as reservoirs and have a history of stocked trout fishing that warranted a (now almost disappeared) refuge hut and a boathouse.

Peat, the sole fuel for the farms that once comprised the only habitation, was sourced here until the Ffestiniog Railway and a modicum of prosperity enabled coal to be used.

Close below is Bwlch y Gorddinan, an ancient frontier, where in winter at least, only the doughtiest of travellers would venture. A close eye would be kept on the skyline here lest the appearance of the wild men of Gwynedd would signal an immediate need to secrete both one's daughters and one's livestock. The present name – Crimea Pass – came into common use when the road was built in the 1850s. To the north of the pass a tree-lined lay-by denotes the site of the Crimea Inn that served as a place of rest and recreation for the men of

the nearby slate workings. Its scanty trade being dramatically augmented in the 1870s, by navvies finding that the cutting of a railway tunnel through diamond-hard rock was a thirsty business.

Sadly, it was here in March 1941 that a Wellington bomber returning maimed from a raid on Occupied France just failed to clear the pass. Five men died on Moel Farlwyd in the ensuing crash, only the rear gunner surviving who to his further terror, was set upon by men speaking some unintelligible tongue, furiously intent on tearing him from his turret with clearly cannibal intent. It was only when Captain Martyn Williams-Ellis, manager of Llechwedd quarry, came on the scene was he reassured that he was about to be rescued not roasted.

Fortunately the 'gravestone' alongside the road has a happier origin. The ground is discoloured by countless rusting hobnails and boot-irons, the incinerated remains of beyond-repair boots from the Blaenau Market Hall factory that serviced the boots of American soldiers assembling for the 1944 invasion of mainland Europe. This factory provided employment in WW2 for women and older men, just as had the American/Welsh funded Pant yr Ynn textile factory in WW1.

The Llechwedd quarry, now famed for its innovative Quarry Tours, captured the carefree Barlwyd

to turn its waterwheels and to generate electricity in the 1908 power station whose immaculate brassbound dynamos still purr forth their volts. Emerging from captivity the Barlwyd finds itself not so much in a valley as in a gully. Nowhere can so much industrial use have been made of so narrow a space with railways stacked three high (the new, stilted road diversion now adds a fourth level).

Incised onto the floor of this gulch, like an unfinished saw-cut is the track-bed of the Ffestiniog Railway reaching to the foot of Lechwedd's incline. Nearby, almost overcome by uncounted millions of tons of rubble, is the site of Dinas station, once the main terminus of the Ffestiniog Railway.

Here, nucleated around the old Rhiwbryfdir farm, was the nascent boom town of Blaenau Ffestiniog. In the event the town developed around the other branch of the railway and the only thing that happened here was the

DAFYDD FRANCIS
DAVID FRANCIS

Y TELYNOR DALL O FEIRION
THE BLIND HARPIST OF MEIRIONNYDD

disappearance without trace of the entire built environment under the inexorable advance of the Welsh Slate Company's tips.

Not only railways but also the quarries were piled three high, for above Welsh Slate was Matthew's quarry and above that Holland's. When they all came tumbling down like the walls of Jericho, landlord Mr Oakeley was left with a quarter of a century's worth of clear up.

When the London & North Western Railway, emerged from its tunnel in 1879 it found the valley so packed with the Ffestiniog Railway and its quarry feeders, that it and its loading sidings had to perch stanchioned on tip-toes above the river,

Literally overarching all was the great Glan y Don viaduct that carried a line from the space-strapped Welsh Slate quarry to a huge tip on top of which was a steam-driven mill.

After being augmented by the drainings of Oakeley quarry the Barlwyd emerges unscathed, to revert to being an ordinary mountain stream.

It accompanies the railway past the extraordinarily-sited Nyth y Gigfran quarry, 'raven's nest', where seemingly none but the foolhardiest of birds would make its home, and on past Samuel Holland's housing sited at the rail side to provide doorstep delivery of coal and such to this then roadless area. At Tanygrisiau the river parts company from the railway leaving it to pursue its own affairs, and drops down confluencing with the Orthin to become the Goedol to serve the lately rebuilt Dolwen Power Station. Under that alias it joins the Bowydd near Cymerau Isaf, an ancient and important forestry centre.

When the augmented river finally reaches the safety of the valley floor, it absorbs the Teigl, and drops all pseudonyms to become the Dwyryd. Although now free to make unfettered meander, it once had one final duty, that of powering the variously wool, timber and slate mill at Rhyd y Sarn.

DWYRYD
10
BLAENAU FFESTINIOG

Sited Mesopotamia-like between the Barlwyd and the Bowydd is Blaenau Ffestiniog, the world metropolis of slate. As recently as the mid 18th century it was a mere geographical location at the very furthest outreach of the Commote of Ardudwy Uwch Artro, where Meirionydd thrusts an enquiring finger into the old Caernarfonshire. In this craggy cwm where an acre of wasteland might support one scraggy sheep, it was said to rain for three-quarters of the year and to snow for the rest. Not too much of an exaggeration since the air of the prevailing south-westerlys, forced between the Moelwyn and the Manod and thrust up almost a couple of thousand feet, had and still has every last drop of moisture wrung out of it like a floor cloth.

Here, since ancient times, slate has been hacked from outcrops whenever a roof needed repairing, not that there were many roofs to repair – and most would be rough-thatched anyway. Commercial

slate extraction was begun by Methusalem Jones, a Caernarfon publican, reputedly guided here by a dream, although more probably by some overhead bar-room remark. What is undisputed is that he established Diffwys quarry around 1760 and, although he and his associates were finessed out of it at the end of that century, his work proved the seed corn for the great Blaenau phenomenon.

Others soon began delvings that would become great undertakings. Thus almost before the echo of the first ring of Methuselem's pick on the rich rock of the Old Vein had faded from memory, Blaenau had outgrown most towns in Wales.

In the meantime, the difficulties facing those early pioneers were immense. The nearest road that might be properly so-called was at Llan Ffestiniog, more than two near-impossible pack-mule miles away. From there, output was carted to the river Dwyryd, along which it was boated to ships riding uneasily at anchor off Ynys Cyngar. However, the slate still had to be sold and record exists of a partner in Diffwys walking to London and waiting there months for the ship to evade the French frigates so that he could turn the cargo into coin and walk sovereign-laden back to Blaenau.

Transport was eased during the first decades of the 19th century by roads built by the quarries. Most have now become main roads, others are disused but make walkable routes. One such track is the steep climb from Pont Fron Goch where it took two prodded and beaten horses in tandem harness to move a mere half ton (500 Kg) up to Congl y Wal. There the lead horse could be unhitched and the load augmented to some 13 cwt (650 Kg) from a roadside dump. Only at Llan Ffestiniog could the load be made up to the cart's one-ton capacity. The route to Llan Ffestiniog is now of course the A470, originally going though Pen y Bont, a diversion that can still be followed.

From 1836 much of the road building was rendered industrially superfluous by the opening of the Ffestiniog Railway, although to the relief of the beleaguered Turnpike Trust, some quarries were slow to use it. After 1863 when the line was steamed, becoming a world centre of narrow-gauge excellence, cartage virtually ceased.

The town proper absorbed three farms: Maenofferen, Gelli, and Bowydd; where life on all three must have been economically parlous unless there was a second income from say, cattle droving or dealing. Maenofferen stood near the present hospital and the name is said to be a

corruption of 'Priest's Stone' and to have a Druidic connotation. In fact it is probably a corruption of Maenofferm 'Farm Stone' since an enormous stone, deposited there by the retreating ice, formed one pine-end of the farmhouse. It had to be blasted to pieces when the farm was demolished. Gelli farmhouse nestles abandoned close under the railway viaduct; Bowydd a little below Pont Fron Goch is still in occupation.

From the 1830s Blaenau developed even more rapidly, the population topping 11,000 with well over 3000 men directly employed in slate working but it was 1844 before the town, hitherto part of (Llan) Ffestiniog parish, achieved its own parochial status. To mark the centenary of the parish church, the great 'Ficar Jacob' (The Very Reverend Dean Ungoed Jacob) commissioned the unique 'Quarrymen's window'. The trees in front of the church were a gift of Sir Thomas Carey Evans, the doctor son of the local GP, one-time personal physician to the Viceroy of India and son-in-law of David Lloyd George.

The daily avalanche of slate-waste that converted the Rhiwbryfdir settlement into a latter-day Pompeii made the Ffestiniog Railway's termination at Dinas redundant as a passenger station, the Diffwys branch then becoming the main line with a station at the foot of the

Maenofferen/Rhiwbach and Bowydd/Diphwys inclines. The station building is now a public lavatory and the marshalling yard a car park, but all trace has gone of the bridge that once carried the lines under High Street. However, the two inclines still make (steep!) footpaths. The present FR/main line station is on the site of the terminus of the Great Western Railway's Bala branch that was Blaenau's third railway and fifth station. The FR had an interchange platform at this station and also a station at Glan y Pwll that gave access to the London & North Western station across the road. The canopy of this FR station served as a grandstand at Manod football ground for many years before being restored to railway use by the Welsh Highland Railway. The buildings and extensive yards of the L&NWR station are now an industrial site. This line was extended in the 1950s to make end-on junction with the ex-GWR line, to maintain access to Trawsfynydd Power Station following the closure of the Bala Branch. The line continues to thread its way though the town passing the site of the surprisingly extensive Manod station where engines were shedded and turned, and where there were sidings to load Graig Ddu quarry trucks onto transporters.

With just two slate quarries left to glare at each other across the Barlwyd divide, the population more than halved and with central heating rendering obsolete the *Tai Uncorn*, the 'Inkpot' houses clinging around a central chimney, Blaenau has had to re-invent itself. This has been aided by the fact that whatever else they have lost, its people have not lost that proud sense of identity forged by harsh unremitting work in a harsh

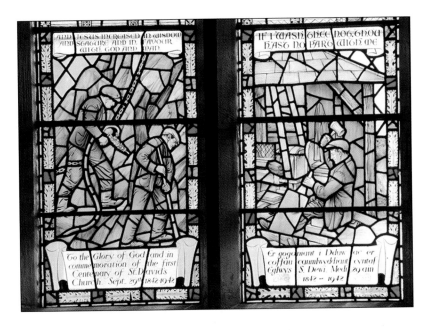

unremitting clime.

There are some half dozen firms working slate in various guises, none are large but all keep ancient skills alive, there are also several non-slate factories and a major tip reclamation is proposed. The main street has an art gallery and shops including a bookshop with a renowned antiquarian department. In what were the "Cocoa Rooms, set up as a teetotal rendezvous to counter the evils of the Demon Drink as epitomised by the Queens Hotel, is the Royal Welch Club. Its name honours that most honourable of regiments, the Royal Welch Fusiliers, under whose Colours so many men of Blaenau fought and died. Unfortunately the Market Hall, that in 1943-44 ensured that Eisenhower's GIs stormed the beaches of Normandy properly shod, no longer fills its erstwhile retail and social functions and is currently seeking a new role.

Almost a dozen modern bands and groups augment the musical tradition of the Moelwyn and Brythoniaid Choirs and the Royal Oakeley Silver Band. Besides artists working in slate there are others working and exhibiting in various media, such as Falcon Hildred in his ex-slate, ex-woollen but still water-wheeled mill, Pant yr Ynn, as well as their doyen, David Nash OBE, RA whose sculptures in wood are exhibited worldwide.

A dearth of toffs with double-barrelled names to match their double-barrelled guns and an absence of game has ended the shooting parties, but Blaenau Ffestiniog remains the power base of the Cambrian Angling Association that has managed sport fishing in the lakes and rivers since 1885.

Mountain-encircled Blaenau offers scope for climbers, its hill-walking potential is legendary and for the more energetic - the annual Moelwyn Peaks Race is now a national event.

DWYRYD
11
MANOD

Mynydd Manod, a bare, bleak volcanic monolith stands with Moelwyn as the Gog and Magog-like guardians over the crescent sweep of Blaenau Ffestiniog. Although granite quarrying is very obvious here, oddly for such a slate-redolent location, it appears to be free of slate-related exploitation. However the slate men, like footpads, robbed the mountain by taking it unawares from behind aided and abetted by the Rhiw-bach tramway that itself hides coyly behind Manod's bulk.

Unlike the main Blaenau workings proudly displaying their tips and tunnellings, the half a dozen infra-Manod extractions lurk like some secret D-noticed activity. Manod (or properly, Bwlch y Slaters) quarry did of course once hold secrets - providing wartime entombment for the contents of the National Gallery, cared for by bewildered curators who hitherto had not realised that intelligent life forms existed beyond Uxbridge.

One highly visible aspect of Mynydd Manod's slate operations is the magnificent cascade of four inclines that

enabled the Graig Ddu slate wagons to reach the railway more than a thousand feet below. Remarkably at the end of each day most of the Graig Ddu quarry workforce also descended by the same route. Not only quarrymen but also stiff-collared clerks and bowler-hatted supervisors careered down the incline rails, precariously perched on skateboard-like 'wild cars'. There are reports of two or even incredibly three men sharing these exiguous vehicles and certainly fathers carried infant children on their laps, as a 'treat'.

Even the schoolmistress of the tiny Rhiw-bach quarry hamlet, having in the morning been hauled up the Rhiw-bach inclines from Blaenau in a slate wagon, would return in the evening down the Graig Ddu inclines by wild car. It is said that young males would lie in wait in the hope of a passion-inflaming glimpse of a stocking-top.

Today the inclines are bare, their formations decayed, the sole clue to their original use are the battered and broken wagons, reminders of derailments long ago. For those climbing these inclines a flat wet area provides a breathing space before addressing the last and discouragingly longest of the inclines. This place is Lefel Oer the site of the main processing area for Graig Ddu quarry. Sadly the elaborate part-underground wheel, shafts and pulleys of its four mills have vanished, leaving just vestiges of the hydraulic arrangements that enabled the waters of Llyn y Manod to be tapped.

Those achieving the final ascent are met at the saddle between the twin peaks of the mountain by utter desolation, where excavation upon excavation has produced a sterile moonscape, where even the most diligent and optimistic sheep would fail to find nourishment.

However with the right conjunction of the elements a great emotional experience can await. Press on to the brow and a vista of the lush meadows of Cwm Machno is revealed, which with luck will be warmed by sunlight shafts. In an instant the cold rocks and rubble beneath one's feet become Moab and Machno the milk and honeyed Promised Land.

Not all the workers went home daily, those living beyond Blaenau made the dizzily elevated barracks their weekday abode, where in winter nights they would lie unwashed in wet clothes in the bone-permeating chill of damp bedding, while the wind threatened to remove the roof and snowflakes drove through the walls' interstices like bullets.

At a lower level and in the lee of Manod, life in the Rhiw-bach settlement was somewhat better. Living en-famille, there was warmth, there were meals, there were dry, flea-free beds and there were proper lavatories. These were built over a brook hygienically sited downstream of the village (calling for a daunting 200 yards sprint on a snow-filled night!). The defect in this otherwise excellent arrangement was that their downstream was the next

village's upstream. Unlike less elevated settlements wages could not be horticulturally augmented since the soil was too barren for cultivation and the climate too severe for livestock. An on-site shop carried a few necessities, but serious provisioning called for a Saturday expedition involving walking three miles of tramway and negotiating four inclines. Fortunately heavy purchases could be left to be brought up (along with the school-marm) on the first rake of empty wagons on the Monday morning. For the younger people seeking entertainment, Blaenau cinemas and dances were equally remote and called for a dauntingly dark and possibly wet return journeys. Allegedly should any Rhiw-bach young lady allow a Blaenau lad to see her home she would be expected to show her gratitude in tangible fashion against the massive head-sheave mounting of the Rhiw-bach incline. It is said that this courtesy sometimes had to be expedited should a search party of brothers be heard ascending the incline.

Although some of the rain that so amply drenches Manod finds its way east to the lush meadows of Cwmmachno, much finds its way to the Dwyryd via the Afon Teigl. Remarkably, this relatively insignificant stream has carved a far from insignificant valley out of the hard igneous rock. This lovely glen, the private world of sheep and rabbits and circling ravens, was once filled with the roar of road tractors laboriously straining at outsized depictions of long-dead monarchs.

Two hundred years ago, before the Teigl valley road existed a magnificently engineered road was built, not by some multinational corporation, sweetened by subsidy and backed by a consortium of banks, but by the modestly pocketed proprietors of the summit-sited Manod slate quarry, precursor to the later Graig Ddu quarry. Though redundant for a century and a half, much of this road that later provided access to Graig Ddu quarry's Lefel Dŵr Oer, survives in good condition, traceable to where is joins the Cwm Teigl road at Llechwedd Isaf. Close by at Brynwennol are the ruins of storehouses where gunpowder was kept after it was no longer available from the Ffestiniog ironmonger.

Ffestiniog, or to give it its modern prefixed form Llan Ffestiniog to distinguish it from the upstart town Blaenau Ffestiniog, was once the premier township of northern Meirionydd. It was an important shoeing station where drovers would overnight their cattle and where traders from Bala

would offer their knitted goods and where timber was bought and sold. Sadly it is now almost a commerce-free zone, bereft of shops, the gunpowder-peddling ironmonger having long gone (presumably to the relief of neighbours!). Some of the inns where travellers having overcome the steep climb from the valley rested and refreshed themselves survive. This climb is now less taxing thanks to the sinuous, coach-friendly turnpike that superseded the old, direct road that can still be traced down to Pont Tal y Bont. Actually the route onward to Bala was even steeper as can be seen today from the trace of the old road that rises where its turnpike replacement branches left at the top of the village. The road from Blaenau has been re-routed several times, once because one William Davies of Caerblaidd objected to the road crossing his land and blew up the Pont Ysgol Newydd bridge over the Teigl.

The war memorial, which honours Ffestiniog's sons who lie in alien fields, has one curious address 'Barracks'. This had nothing to do with quarry or military accommodation, but to premises higher up the street whose yard made it a convenient abode for itinerant vendors with carts. For those living in remote areas peddlers played an important role in the community, extending credit paid off on each weekly call. Despite the area's poverty they did a substantial trade in books. Such peddlers were regarded as 'black sheep', but black sheep in Llan Ffestiniog are now more substantially represented by the famous Pengwern Hall flock.

Standing proud, Llan Ffestiniog church must in olden times have been a heartening beacon to all traversing a then inhospitable landscape. A window enigmatically recalls a daughter and grand-daughter lost on a wartime flight from Lisbon along with actor Leslie Howard. The churchyard views are unrivalled and it is not easy to think of any other vista that one could so untiringly contemplate for all eternity.

DWYRYD
12
THE MIGNEINT

High above on the plateau where a breeze's whim decides if a raindrop is to augment the Conwy or the Dwyryd, is the Migneint; a barren, acidic waste where even bodies of armed men once ventured at their peril. Apart from the risk of being sucked into a morass whilst lost in freezing fog, there were the bandits of Ysbyty Ifan. The Ysbyty being a holy hospice the royal writ did not run, therefore no constable could make apprehension and no miscreant could face earthly justice. In other words an ideal place for vagabonds and cutpurses of every kidney to lodge and lust over their loot. To compound the dangers of this moor, three pillars defined the meeting place of three counties. Apparently any fleeing villain squeezing between the pillars at this point of county conjunction was in such a jurisdictionally indeterminate location as to make arrest impracticable, at least until hunger or a call of nature forced a change of situation.

Today, provided one can dodge the speeding traffic,

the greatest menace comes from importuning sheep anxious to share a sandwich.

Robbers apart, it was not always free of armed conflict. It seems that in Ardudwy a shortage of comely women in the appropriate age-bracket curtailed both recreation and procreation. Accordingly to correct this imbalance a force of mounted men was dispatched to Dyffryn Clwyd, where there were (and still are) many women of uncommon comeliness.

Returning by night with a young woman draped over each saddle pommel a halt was called at break of day to enable the Ardudwy men to appraise their booty. Thus they found themselves at some disadvantage when a pursuing posse from Dyffryn Clwyd caught up with them. The women, as one man as one might say, upped and threw themselves into a nearby lake and drowned. Dyffryn

Clwydians claim they were motivated by shame at their manifest compliance in the proceedings. Men from Ardudwy aver that it was the prospect of the loss of partners so adept in the amatory arts. Whatever, the Dyffryn Clwyd men declared that since the Ardudwyans wished to lie with their women they would see that they did; hence slaying every last man and burying them hard by the lake named, touchingly if technically inaccurately, as Llyn y Morwynion, *'the maidens lake'*. Actually the pun does not quite work in Welsh and the reputed graves are three-quarters of a mile distant, but that has never deterred countless generations of storytellers.

Another legend is that the maidens were from Ardudwy themselves and were rather sensibly taking to the hills to escape from Gwydion the readily dislikeable nephew of Math, the ruler of Gwynedd. In this version, the maidens, fearfully looking behind them, stumbled headlong into the lake. Only one, Blodeuwedd, survived. She was set upon by a sword-brandishing Gwydion who promised her a fate worse than death but presumably to her surprise, turned her unsullied into an owl.

What is fact is that at an open-air poetry festival alongside this lake a young Trawsfynydd farm-boy first used the name that resounds like a trumpet through the Pantheon of Welsh heroes - Hedd Wyn.

Hereabouts are many turgid pools, some of them seasonal, but the brackishness that discourages fish, is no deterrent to birds. Whilst the species are now less varied, red grouse, black cock, wheatear and skylark lurk here as do curlew and snipe, and just occasionally at dusk, the short-eared owl.

Whilst the Llynnau Gamallt drain into the Teigl via Afon Gamallt, these nearby lakelets unite to form the Afon Gam *'crooked river'* well named since it dodges and feints like a fly-half evading an opponent's tackle. The Gam ripples in idle cascades as if savouring its emancipation from its earlier

quarry-wheel toil as it babbles lightly to that lonely outpost Pont Afon Gam. Here it unites with the Cynfal that has made its way from its source, Llyn Dywarchen *'the lake of the turf'*, one of three Snowdonia lakes with this curious name. Although once a trout lake, natural acidity has reduced it to lifelessness.

After their meeting the Gam and the Cynfal, like two schoolboys egging each other on, cast aside their previous tinkling sobriety, conspiring to plunge headlong into the gorge, creating the thundering torrents of Rhaeadr Du and Rhaeadr Cynfal, where in a National Nature Reserve is as fine a display of mosses and ferns as any in Europe, including the antiseptic Sphagnum moss that figured in Huw Llwyd's magical cures.

Then quite suddenly as if tiring of its play, the river takes pause at Cwm Cynfal now a secret cleft of tranquillity, once a tiny slate quarrying community although since devoid of a chapel it cannot be considered even a bona-fide hamlet. In fact the near-healed scars of the mini workings seem to have been cut by ephemeral elves.

Having taken breath in Cwm Cynfal, the river again becomes embroiled with waterfalls, but this time also with a warlock.

Shortly after passing under Pont Newydd the rushing water is defied by a pillar in its midst. This is the Pulpit where sure-footed as a goat, Huw Llwyd declaimed and cast out demons. As a young man Huw had sought fame and fortune in France and Holland with King Billy, he of the Derry siege. Finding neither, he settled down to the life of farmer, poet and wizard at Cynfal Fawr, the building of the present house being attributed to him. Being a seventh son he was blessed with certain insights and powers denied to those lacking the appropriate number of pregenitored male siblings. A poet of some standing, he could cure ailments and foretell events, but it was his power to

detect witches that was his forte.

He travelled confidently since a hastily cast spell would deal with any robbers and one night found himself at an inn at Cerrigydrudion kept by two elderly sisters where apparently guests' possessions were liable to disappear overnight. Awakened by rustling, a Lucifer match revealed two cats rifling his pockets. They scuttled away up the chimney at the sight of his sword but he did manage to

graze the forepaw of one. Next morning only one sister served breakfast, the other being said to be indisposed. Huw demanded to see her and found she had a bandaged hand. Since drawing the blood of a witch would render her harmless, it is said that he cut the hand of the other sister, so neutralising the pair of them. True or not, from the time of Huw Llwyd's visit no guests were relieved of their valuables.

From his deathbed, Huw directed his daughter to cast his book of potions and magic into the pool of Rhaeadr Du. Realising the book's value, she hid it but told her father that she had done his bidding. When she confirmed that it had made splash, he became very angry and told her not to lie. Again she pretended that she had carried out his wish but the third time under the threat of having a spell cast, she did throw the book into the pool. A great hand rose to catch it and it splashlessly disappeared.

The Cynfal flirts briefly with the ancient village of Ffestiniog, then, keeping company with the traces of the old pre-turnpike road, joins the Dwyryd having passed under Pont Tal y Bont. This tautologically named span was part of the early 19th century turnpikery. Prior to this, travellers would have gone straight down to the valley floor where they could cross the Dwyryd by Pont Dôl y Môch where on one parapet there is the footprint outline used to symbolically mark the first step of a long journey. Those wishing to go to Trawsfynydd could cross the Cynfal by Pont Dôl Rhiw Felen. As can be clearly seen from underneath it was widened when it was incorporated into a direct link to Maentwrog. The turnpike via Pont Tal y Bont rendered the Dôl Rhiw Felen crossing redundant, hence it now stands in a field forlornly leading nowhere.

These two bridges, Pont Dôl y Moch, and Pont Dôl Rhiw Felen, were obviously once fords and may have been the origin for the name Dwyryd, *'two fords'*.

DWYRYD
13
CWM ORTHIN

Besides contributing to the Dwyryd, Afon Cwmorthin like the Barlwyd and the Bowydd, had to work for its living. Waters from several lakes and countless streams meet in a hanging valley jammed between Allt y Gefflau and Moel y Hydd/Foel Ddu that is almost entirely filled by Llyn Cwmorthin.

The Orthin's major source is Llyn Conglog the highest lake of its size in Wales, a thousand feet above Llyn Cwmorthin. Conglog, long thought too elevated for good fishing, now has trout in some numbers thanks to a restocking to take advantage of the milder winters of the late 20th century. At one time anglers maintained a boat and boathouse on many of these remote mountain lakes and at some, a hut where shelter could be taken, sandwiches eaten and the size of past catches exaggerated. It is sad reflection on our times that almost all these structures have fallen victim to vandalism.

Other lakes include Llyn Coch, Llyn Cwm Corsiog, Llyn Clogwyn Brith and the curiously timber-dammed Llyn Coed, all once part of Rhosydd slate quarry's extensive water supply. This water having done its duty at Rhosydd ended up at Llyn Cwmorthin, but not before turning the wheel at the little Conglog quarry tight against the head of the valley.

This quaint working, entirely surrounded by Rhosydd territory, was flanked by Plas Cwmorthin, the Rhosydd manager's house and the now ruinous Rhosydd chapel. The potential of this tiny enterprise, at one time worked as a spare time venture by Rhosydd quarrymen, was considered sufficient to justify a three-quarter mile extension to the Cwmorthin Tramway. Its formation largely forms the valley track that except for one bend is in clear view of Plas Cwmorthin. It is said that

each morning the occupants would watch for the postman to appear as he breasted the rise from Tanygrisiau and watch his lakeside progress until he was lost from view at the bend. According to rumour the unsighted postman would then sit and wait knowing that when he failed to re-appear, a maid would be sent to look for him, thus shortening his tedious walk.

Llyn Cwmorthin is a substantial lake despite having been considerably reduced in size by quarry tipping and is regarded (and guarded!) by anglers as useful sporting water. Overlooking the lake is the oft-portrayed Cwm Orthin barracks, actually a row of houses that, according to requirements, could be let either as communal or as family accommodation; the latter use supplementing the numerous quarry-owned houses below at Tanygrisiau.

The lake outfall successively powered the three Cwm Orthin quarry mills, in order to achieve sufficient fall, the last of these had its Pelton wheel in a deep pit driving its machinery by a belt. The quarry itself was almost entirely underground, and on the mountainside above can be seen the cracks in the ground from when chambers underneath caved in due to injudicious working during the 1870s bonanza. It was possibly the most dangerous workplace in the country; those that escaped collapses faced asphyxiation from the fumes of the underground boilers. In the late 20th century it was successfully worked on a modest scale, a battered Landrover carrying away its product from a mill in an abandoned chamber. Regrettably, following a take-over, it was despoiled by ill-considered open casting that destroyed much of the unique archaeology.

At the valley's cusp, the river leaps like an intrepid hang-gliderist down to Tanygrisiau, where it is leated and disciplined in preparation for its duties at the Dolwen power station. The tramway makes a much more measured descent via two inclines which, tasteful though they are, cannot compare for spectacle with the Wrysgan incline formation emerging from a tunnel to drop like a raptor on a rabbit. It connected with the Ffestiniog Railway near the erstwhile Wrysgan quarry manager's house at the far end of the present car park, from where the old FR track bed forms the road to the power station. Even the Wrysgan is outdone by the cascade of inclines that zig their zags from the seemingly stratospheric Moelwyn quarry to join the original FR route (now under water), in front of the present power station. These slate workings were first exploited, (with little success!) by financier Nathan Rothschild, the scars of whose previous searches for copper hereabouts can still be seen. Subsequent slate diggings were more fruitful and here at almost 2000 feet, was not only the water-driven slate mill, but also family accommodation. Here, defying the relentless winds and the all-permeating elements, wives kept house and raised families, sending children (busless!) to school at distant Tanygrisiau. Traversing the quarry area is the extraordinary packhorse route benched out of the hillside, used by Rhosydd quarry to reach the Dwyryd at Maentwrog via Cwm Maesgwm.

Rothschild, in the meantime, had transferred his affections to the Rhiwbryfdir-engulfing Welsh

Slate Company. This company's failure to pay wages was apparently OK, but its failure to pay dividends was a different matter and Rothschild was deposed. Lord Palmerston, who was instrumental in abolishing the Slate Tax thus paving the way for Blaenau's prosperity, replaced him. 'Lord Pam' eventually became Prime Minister and severed his connection with the quarry company. He appears to have retained an interest in slate, since in 1865 when aged 80, he died on a slate-bed billiard table at his home at Brocket Hall, allegedly whilst enjoying the close companionship of an under housemaid.

At Tanygrisiau the river powered a foundry that although never on the scale of the big Porthmadog concerns, was nevertheless an important supplier of slate quarries' engineering requirements.

Llyn Tanygrisiau is the most accessible of the Snowdonia lakes and having been created in the late 1950s, is also the most modern. It forms the lower reservoir for the pumped storage scheme and from here, using 'Off Peak' electricity, water is pumped to fill Llyn Stwlan; a reservoir created out of the little corrie tarn that once fed the water wheel of Moelwyn slate quarry. At times of peak demand the water flows back down, the pumps becoming turbines and the motors generators.

Llyn Tan y Grisiau absorbed Llyn Ceg Twnel *'tunnel mouth lake'* named after the Ffestiniog Railway's Moelwyn Tunnel that was plugged when the lake

drowned a section of the Ffestiniog Railway, which at that time the powers-that-be regarded not as a transport link, but as a plaything. It took one of the longest lawsuits in history to prove them wrong and enable the present Deviation line to be built at a higher level. This of course, involved the Dduallt 'Alpine Loop' where the line climbs in a circle enabling folk in both their first and second childhoods, opportunities to wave twice to each engine driver.

Also now vanished is Llyn Inclein formed by damming Nant Ystradau to power the water wheel that hauled the FR incline used before Moelwyn Tunnel was opened. Later, the stream drove a small slate mill; the FR Deviation now passes through a breach in this dam.

The lake is kept stocked with both Brown and Rainbow trout that seem to thrive on the daily rise and fall in the lake level, although the early morning angler has to be ready to beat a retreat as the power station meets the demand of breakfast kettles and toasters. On the southeast of the lake are the remains of Brooke's stone quarry, one of several in the area that met a need for granite setts and chippings and partly compensated the FR for the early 20th century tapering off of the slate trade. Opposite is the incline formation of the Moelwyn lead and zinc quarry. Both this and the granite working were served by now submersed branches of the FR.

The outflow from the lake augments the Cwm Orthin's waters to conspire with the Barlwyd to become the Afon Goedol to turn the turbines of the new Dolwen Power Station. That replaced the 1899 Yale Electric Power Company's installation that was a pioneering public supplier, and with Cwm Dyli, the only industrial power supplier until the much larger (26Mw) Maentwrog Hydro station came on line in the 1920s. Many of the original wooden distribution poles of both power stations still march across the hills.

DWYRYD
14
PRYSOR

Afon Prysor's main sources are Llyn Conglog Mawr and Llyn Conglog Bach (not to be confused with the Cwm Orthin Llyn Conglog) on a rogue outpost of the Dolgellau Gold Belt south of the bleak though now much afforested Migneint. Nearby is the pathetic little Gefail y Meiners mine where a tiny iron waterwheel pumped through the long deserted nights. Its owner sought gold but would have settled for anything of a metalliferous nature. Where the river flows under the fine 7-arch Cwm Prysor viaduct was the scarcely more successful Prysor mine. A little distance off is the Prince Edward gold mine that was more productive but its scanty revenues cannot have made it a 'Gold Mine' for its optimistic owners. It had a millpond that in addition to its industrial, domestic and sanitary purposes, also provided a pre-breakfast dip for the manager, who having seen to matters here had a daily cross-country walk of a dozen miles each way to oversee Gwynfynydd mine.

The viaduct carried the Great Western Bala to Blaenau branch, perilously perched on a shelf incised into the rock high above the valley floor. Running mostly through barren countryside, it carried more sheep than people and had more stopping places than a city-centre bus.

In the valley below, virtually road-less until the late 1950s, is Castell Prysor, where on a curious natural knoll are vestiges of a Celtic stronghold that once provided bed and breakfast for Edward I. From here the river progresses towards Llyn Trawsfynydd, a 3-mile long reservoir created in 1928 out of a number of small lakes to serve the Maentwrog hydro power station with the regrettable inundation of 18 dwellings and a chapel. Later a heat sink for the nuclear power station, it has become angling water of international standing. The four islands provide a rich bird habitat for curlew, Canada geese, teal, coot, sandpiper, meadow pipit, cormorant, divers, great crested grebe, pied wagtail, meadow pipit, red breasted merganiser and duck of several kinds.

The nearby Trawsfynydd village is in two parts, the 'old' nucleated around the church and the 'new' that grew up around two railway stations. One station was a normal passenger, goods and livestock depot, the other handled the horses, gun carriages, ration carts, ambulance wagons – all the paraphernalia of the troops who marched along the arrow-straight Roman road from here to their camp and firing range at Bronaber. The fine Llys Ednowain Interpretation

Centre was the Temperance Hotel where the officers dined with their ladies, while the rough soldiery caroused and womanised in less refined establishments.

'Traws' remains a bastion of Welshness, its by-pass enabling it to maintain some simulacrum of rural tranquillity. Until the 20th century its most notable son was St John Roberts a Catholic martyr put to death under Elizabeth I when 'Popery' was seriously out of fashion. Curiously, this strangely secular-sounding name was shared by the 19th century divine who, as Ieuan Gwyllt, composed the great Congregationalist anthem *Gwahoddiad,* much sung in these parts.

In 1917 St. John's primacy was eclipsed by a young man, Ellis Humphrey Evans from nearby Ysgwrn farm who, as a soldier in the 15th Battalion the Royal Welsh Fusiliers, submitted a poem Yr Arwr *'the hero'* under his Bardic name of Hedd Wyn to the National Eisteddfod, that due to war-time exigencies was held that year at Birkenhead.

That poem gained him the Chair, the great accolade that entitles recipients to be addressed as Prifardd *'master poet'* to the end of their lives. Tragically his life had already been ended by a shell at Picken Ridge near Passchendaele.

To add poignancy, the ornate Chair that stood empty on that Eisteddfod stage awaiting an occupant who would never be seated in it had been made and presented by a Belgian refugee from the Passchendaele area who had settled in Liverpool. It was a token of thanks for the kindness shown by Liverpool-Welsh people to him and his fellow refugees. By some uncanny prescience it had been finished in unrelieved black.

A statue commemorates Hedd Wyn in Trawsfynydd and on the 75th anniversary of his death, a plaque was unveiled near the site of the dressing station in Flanders where he died. Although he never bore the title Prifardd in life, it and his Bardic name that ironically translates as Perfect Peace, remain in perpetuity, incised on a headstone that stands among the serried ranks of Artillery Wood Cemetery.

The chair – y Gadair Ddu, *'the black chair'*, was carried funereally shrouded in solemn ceremonial cortege from Trawsfynydd station to his birthplace, where it remains flanked by Chairs previously won at local eisteddfodau as an iconic shrine that no true Welsh person can look upon without emotion.

These were not the only untimely deaths. At the end of the Civil War John Morgan, who had been a Captain in the Royalist army abandoned his home known later as Plas Capten and hid in a cave,

but soldiers from solidly Cromwellian Dolgellau flushed him out and shot him. Another 17th century death occurred when a young man Hwfa fell in love with a daughter of Goppa farm, but he being a gwas *farm labourer* marriage to the daughter of a freeholder would have contravened the strict conventions of the time. He was found drowned in one of the pools that later formed the present lake. The daughter died shortly afterwards and her ghost is said to still seek him at the lake's edge.

This tragedy was mirrored a century later when Anne Hugh a lady from London fell for the son of a rather doubtful couple who lived at Bryn Hir (one of the homes inundated in 1928). The couple fearing that this Sais *Saxon* woman would deprive them of an unpaid labourer, commissioned one Jac Pegi to kill her. Having done so, Jac was found drowned in a pool (Llyn Jac Pegi) and shortly afterwards the couple mysteriously perished due it is said to vengeance wrought by Anne's apparition.

Bryn Goleu (on the road up to Ysgwrn) was also troubled by a ghost, eventually laid by paying a lady called Gwenno 50p to exorcise it.

The history of the area goes back beyond historic times as testified by vestiges of Iron Age iron making and of the great Bronze Age beaker find, now replicated at Plas Tan y Bwlch. At Tomen y Mur was stationed a Roman cohort charged with keeping open

the road to *Segontium* [Caernarfon], that given the hostility of both the climate and inhabitants, cannot have been a popular task. The little amphitheatre, their sole source of diversion survives, but the dressed stones of the rest of the fort have vanished to mysteriously reappear in many buildings hereabouts. Nearby was found a wooden page of a Roman book, unfortunately this classicist's holy grail did not carry imperial fiat or dactylic hexameter, but merely the minutiae of a testamentary bequest.

From Llyn Trawsfynydd's dam massive pipes and tunnels lead water to the Maentwrog power station robbing the Rhaeadr Gigfran and Rhaeadr Ddu of much of their grandeur, but the gorge remains a place of dank mysterious beauty entirely taken over by ferns and mosses and the crowding, gnarled timbers of the sessile oaks.

Near the power station, some yards upstream from the present road bridge, where the waters from the turbines are re-united with those that escaped capture, is the 'Green Bridge'. Allegedly Roman, it is in fact a post-Medieval replacement for a ford, Felenrhyd *'yellow ford'*. Here was killed Pryderi, the great ruler of Dyfed, who possibly lived where Narberth castle now stands.

It all started with Gilfaethwy nephew of Math the magician-ruler of Gwynedd fancying Goewin his uncle's favourite foot maiden. It was then usual for such potentates to include in their retinue a girl to support and care for their feet after a long day's marching and magicking. Such young ladies were not regarded primarily as bedfellows, but you may be sure that if they were to fellow any bed it would be their boss's. Gilfaethwy's brother Gwydion devised a plan, devious by even his standards, which would lure uncle Math away, enabling Gilfaethwy to press his attentions on the paediatric lady.

Gwydion told uncle Math that Pryderi had animals in Dyfed called pigs, whose flesh made nice eating and offered to obtain some to grace the Gwynedd regal table. Gwydion marched south with

ten men to Pryderi's court, where he offered twelve white horses in exchange for a like number of pigs. Since his pigs were magic pigs, Pryderi wasn't selling, so Gwydion upped his offer to include golden harnesses for the horses and a dozen fast greyhounds. Pryderi could not resist a special offer and a deal was done.

The trouble was that Gwydion did a spot of magic himself and the horses, harness and dogs vanished at midnight,

106

by which time the pigs and the Gwynedd lads were long gone. In due course a very angry Pryderi travelled north mob-handed.

As Gwydion expected, Math, hearing of this incursion, took a large army to meet the Dyfed men. It being a military matter he left Goewin behind and since he was thought to be too wimpish for warfare, Gilfaethwy was also left.

As soon as Math was out of sight Gilfaethwy had his extremely wicked way with Goewin. This, of course, resulted in Math being far from delighted and he turned both nephews into animals and for good measure impregnated their sister Arianrhod.

Anyway in the meantime the armies had met at Felenrhyd with much bloodshed and Pryderi was slain.

This was not the only slaying near this point. It was customary to appoint a man of good standing to act as a part-time rates collector. Such a man was William Evans of Llennyrch who one evening in November 1831 was returning home from making collections when he was set upon by two men who beat and robbed him. He died from his injuries and a countywide murder hunt was mounted, but although stories are still told of deathbed confessions, the miscreants have never been identified. The spot where he was struck down is informally commemorated a short way up the forest path on the western side of the river, by a tree having the initials 'W E' carved into its bark.

Llennyrch used to be connected with Llech y Cwm by a high-arched bridge over the Prysor, on the ancient route from Llandecwyn to Maentwrog. Under the bridge was a well of allegedly Roman origin and a pool where sheep were dipped. Many years later Richard Evans a descendant of William predicted that he would be the last person to cross that bridge. He died shortly afterwards and immediately after his coffin was carried across it the bridge unaccountably collapsed wrecking the pool and the well. The haunches of the bridge still stand.

DWYRYD
15
MAENTWROG

Having assembled most of its tumbling tributaries, the Dwyryd starts its slow progress along the Vale of Ffestiniog as if a *hiraeth* [longing] for the hills makes it reluctant to forsake them.

Lord Lyttleton wrote of the valley in the 18th century –

'With the woman one loves, with the friend of one's heart, and a good study of books, one may pass an age there, and think it a day.'

Heading this vale that causes poets to suffer a superlatives shortfall, is Plas Dôl y Moch; a fine 17th century house, now an outdoor pursuits centre in which are preserved friezes that depict the ancient tribes of Gwynedd.

At the limit of the Dwyryd's navigable water, is the village of Maentwrog; well known for the export of slate it was also the main trading port of northern Meirionnydd. Goods were originally

shipped and landed at a quay in what became the rectory garden, later supplemented by the Cemlyn Quay and Parry's wharf on the Cemlyn canal that was formed by deepening the Nant Twll Maen. This was the hub of activity and the still extant storehouses were depots for all sorts of exports and imports, including covertly landed wines and spirits. Excise duty made soap smuggling big business and by the time the tax was removed in 1862, one Maentwrog entrepreneur had a distribution network that reached as far as Denbigh. In addition, a quirk in the tax system enabled British salt to be bought in Ireland for a penny per pound and sold in Britain for four pence, creating further smuggling opportunities. It is alleged that since all the local Magistrates were customers, the smugglers if caught would be immune from conviction.

The Llan Ffestiniog merchants would have exported wool from here, indeed there was an early woollen factory at Caen y Coed Isaf powered by the Afon Tafar-Helyg on the site of what had been the first commercial slate quarry in the whole Ffestiniog area.

By the early 19th century slate exports were overwhelming the port, and some half a dozen additional quays were established lower down the river, culminating in the quite magnificent Tyddyn Isa, on the north side upstream of the railway bridge.

Besides its maritime importance, Maentwrog was also on a drovers' and later a Mail coach route gaining prominence in the late 18th century by having a Post Office that handled all Blaenau Ffestiniog mail until a Post Office was opened there in 1840. The village had shops of almost every kind with some half a dozen, including a Co-op, surviving to the mid 20th century. There was never a fish shop, since with an under-bailiffed river teeming with suicidal salmon, a fishmonger would have starved.

Although a notable place of trade, Maentwrog's prime fame is ecclesiastical. The church was dedicated to St. Twrog, who allegedly paused here to remove from his shoe the boulder [Maen] incorporated into a corner of the church.

Since Twrog was not an "Official" saint, the Normans rededicated the church to St Mary, but when rebuilt in its present form, the Twrog dedication was restored, presumably causing some sort of Heavenly crisis of identity. Nearby Glan William the 18th century Plas Tan y Bwlch Dower House lattery housed the rector in a style to which few bishops could aspire. Cytaf Fawr a much more modest abode, had been the traditional rectory, although the parish's most famous incumbent

Edmwnd Prys, lived at Tyddyn Du. This redoubtable Archdeacon collaborated with Bishop William Morgan in his translation of the Bible into Welsh Bible, which was indisputably responsible for the language's survival.

Despite the ecclesiastical pedigree there were crimes, most being riots such as the great rampage of 1762 and those during the harsh winters and failed harvests of the 1790s when rumours of imported grain being hoarded abounded. In 1745 there was a murder, local man Owen Humphrey being slain by John Richard. Since the latter was an incomer his conviction was inevitable, although he may not have been hanged, since death sentences were often commuted to transportation not for humanitarian reasons, but because of a shortage of labour in the colonies. Not so fortunate was Thomas Jones convicted on doubtful evidence for the slaying of Mary Bruton on Manod Mountain in 1898. Colonial transportation no longer being an option, he was hanged.

Plas Tan y Bwlch overlooks Maentwrog like a Gulag watchtower, exactly placed to oversee every aspect of life in the village, every stick of which it once owned. Allegedly, the three non-conformist chapels were sited out of view of the Plas so that tenants attending such places could not be identified by their fiercely Anglican Oakeley landlords.

It is said that had the nazis won the war, the Plas would have been seized, William Joyce (Lord Haw-Haw, the Nazi broadcaster) having taken a fancy to it when staying nearby at Coed y Bleiddiau. Today a sapling wolf preserves Coed y Bleiddau from traitors and safeguards its name *'wolf's wood'*.

At Tan y Bwlch as the area north of Maentwrog bridge is correctly known, the first 'Big house' was the 14th century Bwlch Coed Dyffryn at or near the Oakeley Arms, This was succeeded by Ty'n Nant yr Efail, just behind the present Plas Tan y Bwlch, which was built by the Gruffydd family. William Oakley from Shropshire married the Gruffydd heiress, a wise move since judicious matrimonial alliances had assembled an estate of some 14,000 acres.

William built the Plas' central part and much of the village including the Octagonal horse-whim house on the home farm. More importantly he was responsible for the present road from the Oakeley Arms to Garreg. This cut out the doubtful section that included the lower part of the present Plas drive and went on to Rhyd bypassing Croesor and the appalling wheel-breaker of a track from

Croesor to Nanmor. He also built containment levees to prevent flooding and to coax the Dwyryd into a picturesque meander. He demonstrated his empathy with the village by switching the Plas' allegiance from Llan Ffestiniog parish to Maentwrog by rebuilding the latter's church.

Seemingly, this rebuild was not well done since his son William Gruffydd, who inherited in 1811, had to re-rebuild it! In fact

a great deal of the village that we see today including Glan William and the Oakeley Arms façade is W.G.'s work. Although it would generate wayleave income and boost the quarry royalties he did not support the Ffestiniog Railway proposal since it would wreck his turnpike revenues. He made unreasonable stipulations such as demanding high walls on either side of the track and his death in 1835 undoubtedly facilitated the opening of the line the following year.

Besides the rents, royalties and wayleaves from slate quarrying on its Blaenau land, the Tan y Bwlch estate profited hugely in the mid 19th century from the demands of the Porthmadog shipbuilders. The oak trees being mainly on steep slopes grew into contorted shapes that were often ideal for the making of ship's ribs and many slopes such as those in Coed Felenrhyd were north facing which yielded a tough and durable timber.

After W. G.'s death his widow continued to occupy the Plas, handing over to a cousin's son William Edward Oakeley in 1869. Envious of the big profits his quarrying tenants were making, W.

E. took two quarries into his own hands - regrettably just as the Great Slate Bonanza came to an end. Added to which the third quarry on his land collapsed damaging his two. Unable to obtain cash compensation he took over the collapsed quarry and spent the next quarter century sorting out the mess.

He did much for the village, including rebuilding the church yet again (incorporating exceptional wood-carving by his wife). He built the Plas gateway-bridge, but heavily borrowed, he never built the planned matching east wing that would have given the Plas a more balanced frontage. The house opposite the front gate was the Plas' own Post Office and also still extant on the main road are their sawmill, flourmill and pioneering generator house, all powered by the Nant yr Efail stream. The house across the road was their blacksmith and little way along was the private laundry. The little boathouse handy for the Cemlyn pool, one of the prime fishing sites on the river, housed the Plas spear fishing coracle, built to a Shropshire design larger than the usual Welsh pattern.

The area is renowned for its fishing, now a sport but once very much a necessity being almost the sole source not only of protein but of sustenance of any kind. It is of course nowadays slightly amusing to read of people being so poor that in winter they had to eat smoked salmon!

On a floor flag at Plas is the incised outline of a 38lb fish spoken of as pike from Llyn Mair that is actually a salmon from the Dwyryd. Although the official record stands at some 43lbs, it is rumoured that many larger fish have been caught but by poachers who obviously could not get them weighed. There is a tale that in the 1920s the measurements of a 'hypothetical' fish were sent to a fishing journal that indicated a weight in excess of 50lbs.

Mrs Inge, W. E. Oakeley's daughter, the last chatelaine of the Plas was latterly a sad figure. Long widowed, predeceased by all her children save an institutionalised daughter, she died in 1961. The estate, still entailed from W. E's quarry losses, was broken up. The Plas was briefly held by a Liverpool merchant before being taken over by the Snowdonia National Park as a residential Study Centre. Much restoration has been done by the Park Authorities and the Society of Friends of Tan y Bwlch has been instrumental in the buying back and organising the management of woodland sold off in the 60s. Arising out of this initiative, this part of the Vale has many hectares of other woodland available for recreation.

Besides its educational standing, Plas Tan y Bwlch's packed lunches enjoy some repute carrying on an old tradition as this 1750s account by J. Jackson shows –

Made a visit to Tan y Bwlch. Mrs Griffiths [Gruffydd] *received me with her usual hospitality and cheerfulness both* [of] *which she is amply endowed by nature. I dined and stayed the night there, and the kind hostess pressed me to prolong my visit. – Finding me determined to pursue my route, she resolved upon supplying us with some necessary stores; and upon examining Owen's* [his servant] *wallet* [travelling larder] *– where we had yet a fowl, a neat's tongue, boiled eggs, bara cause* [bara caws – bread and cheese], *she notwithstanding persisted in pressing a large home-baked spiced bun, with some tea and lump sugar into each of my coat pockets.*

DWYRYD
16
PENRHYNDEUDRAETH

This riverside village situated on the spit that separates the estuaries of the Glaslyn and the Dwyryd is appropriately named the *'headland of the two beaches'*. Like all Welsh villages it lays claim to a poet, the 18th century Ellis Wynne, but fame first came here in 1073 when Trehaen ap Caradog the then ruler of Gwynedd repulsed and routed the Anglesey upstart, Gruffydd ap Cynan who sought to take over the territory.

Lime was produced here for the building of Harlech castle, but the traditional occupations were fishing by the men and cockle picking by the women. By medieval times, good agricultural land with little unproductive moor, made this a relatively wealthy area. Its little ports, Aber-iâ where Portmeirion now stands, Borthwen and Abergarfran, as well as a landing place near the present toll bridge, brought travellers and trade.

By the 17th century there were several small estates with houses such as Plas Newydd, another residence of the influential Anwyl family. It is often forgotten how economically beneficial these gentry estates were, with even modest ones having a dozen or more servants, all better housed and better paid than they would have been in almost any

other rural employment.

Industry developed in the 18th century with lead mining at Llanfrothen and copper mining at Rhyd, culminating in Penrhyn's most famous activity, boating down river ever increasing tonnages of Blaenau Ffestiniog slate.

There had been a long history of small quantities of slate being loaded onto coastal vessels at Maentwrog, but by the later 18th century such cargoes were being boated down river to be transhipped into sea going ships. This traffic rapidly developed growing forty fold in the first four decades of the 19th century. Dr Michael Lewis lists over 40 boats (possibly not all in use at any one time). Many were Penrhyn crewed, some boats belonged to a quarry or a landowner; the majority were independent but still usually contracted to one quarry. These slate boatmen or Philistines formed a tight community, jealously guarding a tough but modestly rewarding monopoly; their work ungoverned by clocks was crammed into a fortnightly fury, a week either side of spring tide. Traditionally, boatmen of this sort were part-paid in beer but the Philistines eschewed alcohol so to make up for this fiscal disadvantage, these otherwise law-abiding folk tended to hide clandestine items under return cargoes of coal and so on. In 1745 the authorities noticed that the resident Penrhyn excise man had been in post for 18 years without intercepting a single smuggler. Despite

his pleas that there were no smugglers to intercept, he was ordered to make some arrests forthwith. His Philistine neighbours being many and muscular, this put him in a dilemma but fortunately there was a 'foreigner' trying to break into the trade who could be safely arrested. Regrettably the interloper 'spilled the beans' on the cosy local arrangements; the boatmen escaped gaol but the excise man did not. Actually the most assiduous of excise man would be hard pressed to make

apprehension, since if he was spotted the smugglers knew both estuaries well enough to lure any investigative lawman into whirlpools and quicksand.

By the 1830s the development of Porthmadog had eliminated the transhipments at anchor in the exiguous lee of Ynys Cyngar. With tonnages expanding explosively, agents on the overloaded Dwyryd slate quays were outbidding each other to secure the boatmen's services.

The 1836 opening of the Ffestiniog Railway heralded the end of the boating bonanza although some quarries, especially the then mighty Diffwys quarry, were reluctant to use this clanking modernity. But inexorably, despite both the boatmen and the carters making swingeing cuts in their charges the trade ebbed away, ceasing completely in 1866.

During this time David Williams, the brother of Madocks' agent, John Williams, had prospered. He had become MP for Meirionnydd and having acquired a modest estate near Penrhyn, enlarged it and ennobled the house as Castell Deudraeth commemorating a putative castle of Owain Gwynedd.

Prior to the 1850s, the main road from Maentwrog to the Cob, as still defined by a side road, ran close alongside the foot of the Penrhyndeudraeth hill with little but marsh to the south of it. Williams' draining of the marsh enabled him to create a new road more appropriate to the coaches he still believed would pass through the village and build the present square inspired by Madocks' Tremadog layout.

Although coach traffic remained sparse, this development well fitted the village's new role arising from the newly steamed Ffestiniog Railway introducing passenger services. With Blaenau bursting at the seams, the FR's reduced workmen's fares enabled Penrhyndeudraeth to become a 'Commuter Belt'.

At about the same time, the Cambrian Railways opened, putting Penrhyn and Minffordd in touch with Harlech then still the county town, as well as giving them the two stations they each still have today. A roadway incorporated into the main line's Briwet Bridge subsumed David Williams' ferry. In compensation for the loss of ferry revenues, Williams was allowed to collect bridge tolls (as his heirs and successors still do). These improved communications united the communities on the two sides of the river and joined up the river-divided parishes of Llanfihangel and Llandecwyn and were also partially responsible for the siting of the Ffestiniog Union Workhouse at neighbouring Minffordd.

Cooke's Explosives was established in 1884 to provide gunpowder for the quarries; its office being on the site of the Nyth y Gigfran Inn where southbound travellers had awaited the ferry and northbound ones recuperated from its rigors. The works closed in 1995 to become a nature reserve, the famed haunt of nightjars. The Garth quarry, opened to meet the Victorian demand for granite setts, now produces road stone. Stone is worked in another sense by Howard Bowcott, rightly famous for his assemblages that break new ground in the conceptual use of slate as a medium for three-dimensional art.

In line with the current trend to exchange picks for pixels, an important employer is now the headquarters of the Snowdonia National Park but this is eclipsed by the acknowledged main 'industry'- Portmeirion. This waterside creation stands on an ancient boat building and cockling creek (the present hotel

is on the site of the quay and a foundry). Begun in the 1920s, it was concocted from bits of buildings from all over Europe. Opinions differ as to the appropriateness, of this 'rescue home for fallen structures' but it certainly reflects the eccentricity of Clough Williams-Ellis whose life's work it became. It has in latter years become one of the best-known places in north Wales with castles and beaches being ignored to visit this unique confection.

Not far away is Penrhyn Isaf farm where one hot summer's day in 1812, Thomas Edwards a labourer known as Hwntw Mawr (*'the big Southerner'*) noticed while working on repairs to the Cob that the entire family were harvesting a field. Having apparently overheard that the farmer, John Roberts, had sold cattle the day before, he entered the clearly deserted house to seek the proceeds. He found the cash without difficulty but was seen by a servant, 18-year old Mary Jones, who had been sent back to the house to refill the ale jug that had been drunk dry in the heat. Edwards killed the girl and hid the money in a dry-stone wall and returned to his work.

When the body was discovered, someone recalled seeing Edwards in bloodstained clothes. A posse soon found both the booty and the murderer who was roped to await the constables. Unguarded he escaped and crossed the estuary where he was eventually apprehended and taken to Dolgellau in irons fashioned by the local blacksmith. Tried and condemned at the Assize, he was hanged and his unusually tall skeleton is reputedly still used in Liverpool Medical School. This murder blighted many lives; the shock killed the victim's uncle and her father suffered an incapacitating seizure, and Hwntw Mawr's wife in Amlwch is said to have died of shame. The unfortunate Mary Jones is buried in (Old) Llanfrothen churchyard.

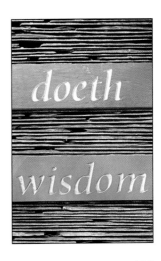

doeth

wisdom

DWYRYD
17
TALSARNAU & LLANDECWYN

This lesser-known south side of the Dwyryd estuary counterpoints some of the features of the opposite shore. It too had a part in the slate traffic (and the smuggling) most of the slate boats being built on this side of the river where many of their two-man crews lived. Although these small single-masted vessels were known to carry about 6 tons and are depicted in several works of art, details of their construction had been long lost until a 1980s tidal quirk exposed an almost complete example in the salt marsh.

Talsarnau is the main village of several settlements in two linked parishes one of which, Llanfihangel y Traethau *'St Michael of the Beaches'*, was once very large and extended on the north side of the river to include Minffordd and most of Penrhyndeudraeth. Similarly the other parish,

Llandecwyn, included the rest of Penrhyndeudraeth. This trans-fluvial confusion was compounded by some land at Nanmor near Beddgelert being an appendage of Llanfair parish south of Harlech where a church door was named *Drws Gwŷr Nanmor 'door of the Nanmor men'*. In addition a tract here at Ynys belonged to Beddgelert Priory.

There was a ferry near the present Briwet Bridge but for most crossings its use entailed a long detour with sandbanks and rip tides making it almost as unattractive as a low-water wade. Besides which, at high tide, Llanfihangel church was almost entirely cut off.

Thus for many, churchgoing involved a dangerous expedition; in fact in 1844 a Colonel Le Clare was so relieved that his family reached Talsarnau in safety that he presented a bell to the then newly re-built Harlech church. Not all were so fortunate as on one occasion some parishioners of the Nanmor outpost, returning from the obligatory Easter attendance at Llanfair, were all drowned.

In the 1750s a Mr. Jackson, a guest of Mr Wynn at Maes y Neuadd (now an hotel) gallantly escorted two ladies, their servants and guides across both estuaries to Pren-teg. Despite a storm, the

tide having risen, and the guides refusing to return, he managed to re-cross the Glaslyn, but got into serious difficulties on the Dwyryd. Having lost his horse he crawled ashore (possibly at Llechollwyn) soaked and half drowned but could get no help from the cottagers who asserted that any person who could cross the river in that sort of weather must be in league with the devil.

Actually one could well face drowning without venturing onto the Traeth. In 1927 a Mr Solomon Jones, trapped by a flood in Talsarnau School, rang the bell to announce his survival and summon rescue (the bell has now been re-hung at the Community Centre).

The repeated crossings implicit in parochial care meant that acceptance of clerical incumbency called for the dedication of a Kamikaze pilot. This may be why at one time neither church had an actual vicar, the joint living being held by the Dean of Bangor, who employed a curate who paradoxically resided at Penrhyndeudraeth the other side of the river! Like several predecessors and successors, the unfortunate young man eventually perished in transit. However, one notable cleric to cross unharmed was Archbishop Baldwin who traversed both estuaries in 1188 accompanied by Geraldus Cambrensis, Archdeacon of St David's, in the course of a 'whistle stop' tour of Wales recruiting for the Third Crusade.

It is not known which route they took; they might have taken the 'narrow' crossing close to the present bridge or from Llechollwyn to Aber-iâ where the domes of Portmeirion exotically glow. It is most likely that they went from Talsarnau to

Abergarfran via Ynys Gifftan, although reaching this island, whose name derives archaically as *'central island'*, would then have been more difficult even on horseback than it is now, since until the 18th century, the main course of the river flowed south of it. They would have employed a guide; possibly identifying him by the white horse sign such as was still displayed outside guides' cottages until comparatively recent times.

Very much extant is the Ship Aground public house that takes its name from the retirement home of Captain John Jones, a naval officer who fought the insurgent American colonists in the 1770s and went on to fight the French with equal distinction.

Llanfihangel church standing on a knoll has a perfectly circular 'Llan' enclosure, its size suggesting that it conforms to the traditional Celtic dimension of the reach of a span of oxen from the altar's site. Surrounded by a fine boundary wall lined with Yew trees, it has the allegedly earliest extant standing grave-marker in Wales. Here are graves of countless Captains who having crossed their Last Bar and met the Great Pilot face to face, find oak-encased rest in the comforting soil of their native Cantref, epitaphed in their mother-tongue, rather than in un-coffined anonymity in the chilly depths of the Southern Ocean.

The gem of the adjacent village of Ynys is Tŷ Gwyn y Gamlas *'the white house on the canal'*. This three-storey warehouse that is served by a canal from the estuary channel, acted as a port for Harlech and was the supply point for the building of Harlech Castle. It is said that there was a tidal mill on this site but no evidence has been found to substantiate this. A modern sluice here protects a large area of Morfa Harlech from inundation.

There were three boatyards, one here at Ynys one at Llechollwyn and a third at Carreg y Ro. At Llechollwyn, once a crossing point, the road runs down into the water and although on a good day there is a fine view across the estuary to Portmeirion, with the wind whipping up the waves it must have taken considerable resolution and firm belief in predestination to commit oneself to the waters. Llechollwyn has a particularly fine *cwt mochyn* [pigsty] of unusual pattern similar to one near the church. In economically marginal times, pigs were an important resource and deserved, and invariably got, appropriately superior accommodation.

Whereas Llanfihangel is very much a maritime parish, and south of the river at least, a low-lying and far from prosperous one, the

corresponding part of its linked neighbour Llandecwyn is less marginal, ruggedly mountainous and in many ways almost an inland area. Its big house is Glyn Cywarch the seat of the Ormsby Gores (later the Lords Harlech).

Unlike many coastal churches, the church of St Tecwyn does not cringe from heathen invaders but stands defiant and proud, proclaiming the Faith of its founder. Now quasi-disused, it is retained and maintained by a trust affiliated to the Small Pilgrim Places network as a place of private prayer and tranquil contemplation where an icon depicts the three Archangels inviting the traveller to sit and - *Listen to the silence.*

To stand among the graves on the close-cut sward and watch the sun eclipse itself behind the loom of Llŷn is one of life's great experiences. It is unimaginable that there can exist as sublime a place to lie and await the Last Trumpet's summons.

The old coach road from Harlech to Maentwrog passes the church gate, but since the traffic now uses the modern road, the old route has become an inconsequential lane, in parts a rocky challenge to even a 4 x 4. It is truly a place of tranquillity where the tiny inn, now functioning as a summer teashop, crouches ready to encounter the winds of winter like a sheepdog eyeing a recalcitrant ewe.

Like all parishes Llandecwyn received bequests from time to time, but there is one bequest it did not receive. In 1769 a Mr. Henry Poole died leaving in his will £5 to this church but the records show that - *Due to the insolvency of the person to who it was lent* this sum was never received!

Hereabouts is a plethora of lakes; the largest Llyn Tecwyn Uchaf, now a reservoir, was the lair of a herbalist and putative witch called Dorti. Prior to the 19th century Poor Laws affording some relief, the plight of a woman on her own was parlous in the extreme. Hijacking a well or cultivating a herb garden gave the opportunity to make ends meet by peddling cures, but success invariably invited satanic attribution. Although Dorti's herbal remedies were renowned, she became suspected of poisoning cattle, a sure sign of witchcraft. Rather than put her to death out of hand, the good people of Llandecwyn being a fair-minded lot, decided to test her infernal credentials by 'casking' her, i.e. rolling her down a steep slope in a barrel with long nails projecting inside. This was a no win situation. If she survived then she was clearly a witch and put to death; if she failed to survive,

then it was a case of 'Oops sorry, you can't have been a witch after all'. Since she was not a witch she failed to survive and her body was cast into the lake.

Her spirit was said to rise from the lake to menace passers-by who could only safeguard themselves by adding a stone to her memorial cairn. Unfortunately since the cairn vanished during one of the lake's several enlargements, the modern traveller must risk a ghostly encounter.

A quarter the size but more beautiful, certified spectre-free and allegedly with trout and perch that are both numerous and gullible, is the heavily be-lillied Llyn Tecwyn Isaf. A little distance away is Llyn Caewych and further off Llyn Eiddew Mawr, that like its tiny sister-lake Eiddew Fach, has signs of ancient settlement.

High above is Llyn Du and amid more evidence of ancient settlement is the curious horseshoe-shaped Llyn Dywarchen where, on a magnificently engineered road, carts carried away the manganese dug to meet the late 19th century need to harden the armour of the Dreadnaughts.

On a rocky eminence is Bryn Cader Faner, the *Crown of Thorns*, one of the most striking of British prehistoric monuments, and rightly considered the 'Stonehenge of Wales'. Although due to age, injudicious investigation and vandalism only about half the slate slabs remain and are now truncated to perhaps half their original height, it is an impressive sight. Obviously a burial place, was it a necropolis serving many generations or a mass interment from some frightful pestilence or genocidal incursion? Or could it memorialise to the end of time some mighty but sadly Homerless Agamemnon who once proudly bestrode this, his fiefdom?

The Cader takes us back possibly four millennia but high above on Diffwys time reaches back further still. The summit has, as if by a giant's jackplane, been shaved billiards-table flat by the ice floe leaving a mini-plateau to be bestrewn with boulders when the glaciers retreated during the last time we had global warming.

DWYRYD
18
YNYS CYNGAR and BORTH Y GEST

At Ynys Cyngar, where the waters of the two rivers combine, a boat could squeeze tight against the shore in what was not so much a bay as a slight indentation in the coastline. Here some shelter could be clawed from the worst of the southwesterly gales and Atlantic waves that roll unchecked from Venezuela.

Although they may not pre-date north Caernarfonshire shipments, some of the very earliest shipments of slates took place here, carried in baskets by the slate men and their families from tiny nearby diggings such as Bron y Foel.

When in pre-Porthmadog days the Dwyryd trade developed, the Philistines would bring their little boats alongside sea-going ships bobbing at anchor here. Slates would be passed one by laborious one, to be painstaking stowed cushioned with bracken for voyages to far distant destinations, the whole procedure taking up to two weeks. Perhaps less tediously, but certainly more heroically, gravestones and even larger slabs were transferred from one heaving vessel to the other slung precariously from a jury-rigged spar. In exchange, the

river craft would take on goods for Maentwrog, occasionally including some of a seriously clandestine nature that might almost outweigh the legitimate cargo.

Later, when Porthmadog had become a relatively major port packed tight with vessels, Ynys Cyngar was where ships would wait tide and turn to enter the crowded harbour. Many of these vessels would have been among the more than 260 built at Porthmadog and Borth-y-gest, and most of the rest would have been built at Pwllheli or elsewhere on Cardigan Bay. Overwhelmingly, they were locally owned and locally insured, manned by locally born and locally trained seamen.

Outward bound from Porthmadog, groaning with cargo, having close hauled past posh Moel y Guest, abode of ships' captains, managers, agents and all those that had made it or pretended to have made it, vessels would reach and round Ynys Cyngar. This and the rocks of Llŷn might well be the last sight of land until Cape Horn or the Cape of Good Hope broke a distant horizon. Or, in all too many cases, the last sight of land ever. For although Welsh ports were remarkably free from 'coffin ships' – aged, rot-ridden vessels dispatched overloaded in the hope that they would be lost with their over-insured cargo - seafaring was still a perilous profession. Nor were losses confined to distant, unfamiliar waters, the prevailing wind made the whole of the north of

Cardigan Bay a lee shore.

Although from the 1840s onwards the Baltic and the Hanseatic ports were favoured destinations for Porthmadog ships, it was in the long haul that they excelled. Early steamers were such prodigious consumers of coal that until quite late in the 19th century they could not undertake extended voyages without bunkering en-route. Thus for transatlantic and Antipodean destinations sail held sway and Porthmadog was very much a sailing ship port. Besides which the steamers' higher freight rates did not attract shippers of non-urgent, non-perishable cargoes such as slate and steamship owners were reluctant to put up with the extended loading times of slate cargoes.

Thus the sailing ships sailed on, the Captain or, as his articles would have it, 'Master under God' watching turn about with the Mate would like the two hands, a cook and a boy, face days without hot food, weeks in wet clothes and wet beds, battered by a relentless, Antarctic-chilled sea. Many young Porthmadog men to whom Llandudno would be as exotic as Xanadu, would be familiar with Valparaiso, and Captains navigated to New South Wales with fewer misgivings than to "old" south Wales.

Slate was not the only export. Emigrants enacting Ford Maddox Brown's emotive painting were carried to America in craft as small as 100 tons to find their fortunes among the slate of Vermont, New York or Pennsylvania, or even to Patagonia to seek a better life in the Chubult valley or ride herd in Cwmhyfryd shadowed by the Snowdon-like Andean peaks.

Less traumatic, but possibly involving equally emotional partings, were the trips made by teenage girls leaving their native land to dwell Ruth-like amidst the alien corn of below-stairs Belgravia to await their guardsman-guised Boazes. [Ruth 2-8]

Most of the ships built at Porthmadog were mixed square and fore-and-aft rig, designed to run well before the wind yet able to close haul and manoeuvre in tight ports and tiny creeks. This eventually culminated in three-masted schooners with square sails on the foremast supplementing the usual fore-and-aft sails that became known as 'Western Ocean Yachts' which, as the sea-trade in slate tapered off, became increasingly involved in the Newfoundland and Labrador salt cod trade.

The last of these to be built at Porthmadog and the last cargo-carrying sailing ship of any consequence to be built in Wales was the *Gestiana*, launched in 1913 from the yard of David Williams, the last and some say the greatest of the Porthmadog Master Shipwrights. As if to serve notice that sail was in its twilight, it was lost on its first voyage when driven ashore in Nova Scotia, fortunately without loss of life.

One way or another sail held anachronistic sway at harbours such as Porthmadog well into the 20th century, even receiving something of a boost for coastal work during WW1. It was believed, with some truth, that sailing ships were less likely to be sunk by U-boats, either because commanders felt a nostalgic chivalry towards sail or perhaps were reluctant to expend a torpedo that was worth considerably more than the target.

The switch from wood and sail to steam and iron dramatically reduced the dangers of seafaring. No longer did seamen have to shorten sail clinging to lofty spars in winds of speeds totally

unforeseen by Admiral Beaufort. Steam enabled ships to power themselves clear of shoals and lee shores. An aged steamer might need more power to pump the ship than to drive it, but would be immune from the dramatic failures of rotting timber. Steamers ended their days empty and unmanned in the breaker's yard rather than sharing a seabed grave with their cargo and crew.

Steam meant heat to wash and to dry clothes and eventually

to heat quarters. Iron doors kept forecastles dry and safeguarded galley stoves from washout. Lighting no longer depended on swinging oil lamps.

Despite Porthmadog being so sail-orientated, steam ships did round Ynys Cyngar; especially the weekly coasters bringing sugar and soap, cakes and corn flakes to the shops of Porthmadog and Blaenau from Liverpool wholesalers. The cost and unreliability of rail freight gave the steamers a competitive edge right into the 1930s when they had to give best to not trains but motor lorries. Some commercial shipping continued into the mid-20th century; one unusual late survivor being the steamer Florence Cooke owned by Cookes Explosives of Penrhyndeudraeth that carried products that rail, road and other ship owners understandably shunned.

Now navigation is almost totally recreational with every sort of craft from sailing skiffs to twin-screw peripatetic palaces jostling for berths. Vessels no longer determine their position by guess and by God, but by satellite. On land, Morfa Bychan is crossed burdened not with panniers but golf bags. The narrow gauge railways carry passenger numbers unimagined in their heyday. Houses rather than crops fill the fields and food comes not from ploughed furrows but supermarket shelves.

Tourism is now firmly established and the extraction of money from visitors' pockets is practiced with as much skill as was once employed in extracting slate from the quarry faces. Despite the cost and climatic attractions of holidaying abroad, right along the coast of Llŷn, cars and caravans abound and a beach hut sells for as much as once did a castle.

Although those now crossing the Traeth Mawr no longer have to heed the Penamser *'the end of time'* bell, rung to denote the last chance to horseback-wade the estuary ahead of the incoming tide, the summer jams on the Cob can make the transit equally protracted.

List of Photographs

COVER

Front
Yr Wyddfa - Snowdon, the source of Afon Glaslyn
Afon Colwyn – north-west of Beddgelert

Back
Afon Cynfal
Ynys Cyngar at mouth of Afon Glaslyn

AFON GLASLYN

AFON DWYRYD

Acknowledgements

It has taken nearly three years to compile the photographs and research the tales for this second rivers book, and without the assistance of many people who have contributed facts, stories and suggestions for places to visit, it would have been much the poorer. Farmers have gladly given permission for Jean to photograph on their land and have often added to the fund of stories; others have again lent precious, long out-of-print volumes. Jean has appreciated the special people who accompanied her on explorations of the huge area covered by these two magnificent rivers and also those who have given her of accommodation. Alun in his wide travels has met nothing but kindness and a determination to assist. As with the first Tales book, both have made many new friends.

Hugh Atkinson & Neville Jones – Llechwedd
Audrey Aspin – Penrhyn Hospital
Sonja Benskin-Mesher
Michael Bewick & Nick Golding - Tan-Yr-Allt
Rob Bishop – Train Driver of "Blanch"
Howard Bowcott
Spomenka Chekerevatz
Dominic Clare
Linda Clare
Peter Crew
Dafydd & Kathryn Davies – Fron Oleu Farm
Eifion Davies - Porthmadog Marine Museum
Liz Dawson – Hafod Pengwern
Margaret Dunn
Tara Winterton – Canoeists
Nuala Dunn – Canoeists
John Elwyn Evans
Gwilym & Phyliss Evans – Gelli Farm
Emyr Evans – RSPB
Charlie Falzon
Pete Firth & Liam Flemming – Kayakers
Emily Fry – Steam Train Assistant
Roger & Barbara Gauler
Rev. Eirlys Gruffydd & Friends of Tan y Bwlch
Margaret Gruffydd
Falcon Hildred
Julie Hodgson
Tony Hodgson
Shelagh Hourahane
Eric Jones - Mountaineer/Base-Jumper
Griff R Jones

Sally Kemble
Jane Lloyd-Francis
Andy McLauchlin
Gay & Gary Morgan - Climbers
David Nash
Tina Neal
Keith O'Brien
Darren Osborne
Andrew Oughton & the Staff of Plas Tan y Bwlch
Steffan ab Owain
Tudur Owen
D John Paul
Maggie Pendrell
Dafydd Phillips–Harbour Master Porthmadog
Sheila and Terry Potter
Melody Preston – Warden Dewi Sant
Morwen Pritchard – Head Ysgol Croesor
Rupert Pullee - Pen y Gwyryd Hotel
Glyn Roberts – RSPB
Martyn Roberts – McAlpine
Carol Shearman
Roy Sloan
David Smith - Warden Craftwyn Centre
Angela & Bill Swann
Nel Thomas – Penrhyn Isaf
Ariadne Van Den Hof
Dafydd Walters
Jane Whittle
Gerald Williams – Yr Ysgwm
Ysgol Croesor Pupils & Teachers

A very special thanks:

To Chris Terrell for the excellent maps
To Twm Elias for the Foreword and for his unfailing help and wise counsel and to the late Merfyn Williams, who, with Twm Elias, was responsible for the concept of the book in the first place.
To Prifardd Myrddin ap Dafydd for encouragement
To Emrys Evans for his expert advice on the various sources of the Dwyryd
Last but not least Cati the Dog, Jean's loyal photography assistant